# DAD
# JKES

## That's How Eye Roll

# BART KING

Art by Jack Ohman

**GIBBS SMITH**
TO ENRICH AND INSPIRE HUMANKIND

To Sheila, who loved words, words, words.

First Edition
24 23 22 21 20          5 4 3 2 1

Published by
Gibbs Smith
P.O. Box 667
Layton, Utah 84041

1.800.835.4993 orders
www.gibbs-smith.com

Designed by Michel Vrana
Printed and bound in China
Gibbs Smith books are printed on either recycled, 100% post-consumer waste, FSC-certified papers or on paper produced from sustainable PEFC-certified forest/controlled wood source. Learn more at www.pefc.org.

Library of Congress Cataloging-in-Publication Data
Names: King, Bart, 1962- author. | Ohman, Jack, illustrator.
Title: Bad dad jokes : that's how eye roll / Bart King, Jack Ohman.
Description: First edition. | Layton : Gibbs Smith, [2020] | Summary: "A goofy, breezy book celebrating Dad Jokes and word play-for your favorite punster."—Provided by publisher.
Identifiers: LCCN 2019028951 | ISBN 9781423652922 (paperback) | ISBN 9781423652939 (epub)
Subjects: LCGFT: Puns.
Classification: LCC PN6231.P8 K56 2020 | DDC 818/.602—dc23
LC record available at https://lccn.loc.gov/2019028951

# Contents

# FOUR WORD

It's a Dad joke!

# Dad Jokes FAQ

*"I am convinced that the only people worthy of consideration in this world are the unusual ones."*
*—The Scarecrow, in L. Frank Baum's The Land of Oz*

## WHAT'S A DAD JOKE?

**A lot of people brag that their parking skills are unparalleled, but I can back it up.**

Sorry! That was an example of a Dad joke.

Basically, anytime someone makes a corny, adorable joke (often a pun), that's a Dad joke.

## BUT AREN'T MOMS DELIVERING FRESH CHUCKLES ON A DAILY BASIS?

Absolutely! It's unfair that these are called "Dad jokes."

However, like Mom jeans, Dad jokes are not gender-normative. People of all ages and gender identities can and do use them. Kids can make Dad jokes, too. And I should point out that the Dad joke doesn't even rank that high in the Hierarchy of Family Humor. It goes:

5. Dad joke
4. Grandma bon mot
3. Cousin quip
2. Uncle wisecrack
1. Mother-in-law one-liner

## SO IF I DON'T HAVE TO BE A DAD TO MAKE A DAD JOKE, WHY THAT NAME?

Throughout history, women have generally been denied opportunities to freely express themselves, and that includes their humor. I'm speculating that dads got to "brand" Dad jokes first, and the name stuck.

The irony is that women often have a relatively larger area of the brain's left prefrontal cortex than men, which is the area devoted to speech production. This would suggest that women would be *more* likely to enjoy wordplay, and thus, these *should* be known as Mom jokes.

But regardless of one's gender identification, it's easy to get hooked on the Dad joke lifestyle. And wonderfully, this lifestyle can be passed on to others. It's sort of like a zombie contagion, but in a good way, where instead of undead zombies, you get people who are a little dad inside.

True Story: My young niece woke up, sat up, and hit her head on the bunk bed bottom. "Bonk," said her dad. "Is that why it's called a bonk bed?" she asked.[1]

## WHY WOULD I WANT TO MAKE A DAD JOKE?

If you enjoy making your friends, colleagues, and loved ones wince, grimace, squirm, flinch, groan, or make credible threats of violence, then Dad jokes are for you.

---

**1.** This same young niece once wrote a card to me addressed to "Uncool Bart," and I've never stopped being impressed by that.

## THAT'S JUST . . . WEIRD. CAN YOU BE MORE SPECIFIC ABOUT WHAT MAKES A JOKE A "DAD JOKE"?

Any humor that seems silly or obvious or potentially annoying is popularly defined as a Dad joke. Since they often rely on word-play or puns, the humor comes from using words with more than one meaning. So this is not really a Dad joke:

**Q. Where would we be without humor?**
**A. Germany.**

But these would qualify:

**People who buy season tickets are wasting their money. I'm enjoying winter for free.**

**For Halloween, I'm putting up a sign advertising "FREE CORPSES." (It'll be a dead giveaway.)**

**SERVER: Sorry about your wait.**
**DAD: Are you calling me fat?**

Dad jokes should be inclusive, appropriate, and non-offensive. They aren't religious or political, and they rarely have any reference to death or violence. Instead, concentrate on trivial and embarrassing humor. If you order eggs at a restaurant, and the server asks how you like your eggs, politely say, "I don't know, I haven't gotten them yet." [2]

And please remember, a Dad joke is never, ever pun-ographic.

---

**2.** Note: As with all dad jokes, never do this without an audience of friends and family who can be mortified on your behalf. Otherwise, you will seem like an insane jerk.

### SO DOUBLE ENTENDRES OR DRUG REFERENCES —

Can't be Dad jokes.

### BUT AREN'T JOKES LIKE THESE SO DUMB, THEY'RE SORT OF AN INSULT TO PEOPLE?

You might annoy, vex, or otherwise aggravate your audience, but you'd never *ever* insult them. That'd be mean! Remember, by definition, Dad jokes are not mean. (They are not sarcastic, either.)

A Dad joke is fundamentally a force for *good*.

**FATHER: I have a dad bod.**
**KID: Nah, it's more of a father figure.**

Think of it this way: Comedians agree that most humor makes fun of someone or something—with the general exception of puns and wordplay. Of course, there are exceptions to that exception, like when Carolyn See said that her mother "had an even disposition—evenly bad." And sure, if your friend said that a certain team would win the big game, but then it lost, you could say, "Nice prediction, Nostradumbass." Those *are* puns, but since they're insulting puns, they're not Dad jokes.

So to clarify, not all puns are Dad jokes, and not all Dad jokes are puns.

### BUT THERE IS SOMETHING INSULTING ABOUT A PERSON TELLING A DAD JOKE THAT THEY KNOW ISN'T FUNNY, RIGHT?

Ah, now here's the secret about Dad jokes. Sometimes the joke *isn't* the joke. Instead . . .

Sometimes, the joke is that you're willing to make the joke.

4

Sometimes the joke is the outrage that the joke provokes.

And sometimes the joke is that someone gets so worked up about the joke, they tell *you* what a mistake the joke was, even though you already knew that when you told the joke!

**"I was named after Harriet Tubman."**
**"Mom, your name is Sofia."**
**"Yes, but I was named AFTER Harriet Tubman."**

## GAH. I DON'T SEE WHY I SHOULD DEVOTE ANY MORE TIME TO THIS.

That wasn't even a question, but I'll still answer it. At its most basic level, a Dad joke is an affirmation of life and love. It's your way of saying, "Look, I care so much about you, I'm willing to take time to torture you with my so-called humor." Dad jokes can . . .

1. Defuse tense situations.
2. Break the ice.
3. Theoretically entertain people. (If not your audience, then at least *you*.)

**"I can win any staring contest."**
**"So you're the—"**
**"Stare Master. I can also put my wallet in either one of my back pockets."**
**"Please don't say it—"**
**"I'm am-butt-dextrous."**

The world is a stressful place, and Dad jokes give us a cozy, good-natured comfort zone. So while Dad jokes are not cool, they *are* awesome. Remember, the great writer Terry Pratchett said, "There is never a bad time for a pun."

## "NEVER"?

Okay, Joe Berkowitz has pointed out that very few puns are made at funerals.

Hang on, I just found that entire Terry Pratchett quote. It goes:

> 1. There is never a bad time for a pun. There's also never really a good time for a pun.
>
> 2. You might as well just stay braced for a pun at all times, and ride them when they come with as much grace as you can manage.
>
> 3. Finally, the fact that you can replace "pun" with "disaster" in these statements says a lot about the human race.

## THAT'S NOT EXACTLY AN ENDORSEMENT, IS IT?

Yeah, but Mr. Pratchett was just having a bit of fun. After all, he once wrote a book featuring a guide who was a yellow talking toad who was feeling unwell. The toad's followers had to "follow the yellow sick toad."

And even if we accept a pun as a mini-disaster, it can *still* create community. Either everyone laughs together at your joke (yay) or your audience is united in hating you. (Not yay, but hey . . . community!)

Finally, a warning:

Reading about Dad jokes is like eating corn chips—great at first, but the more you do it, the worse you feel. Please exercise restraint in the consumption of this book.

# On Courage

*"Every joke is a tiny revolution." —George Orwell*

I salute you for your courage.

Telling jokes requires bravery. Any time you say something like "If your friend tells you to jump off the dock, that's pier pressure," there will be people who let you know they are not amused.[1] In fact, there must be a lower ratio of positive feedback for Dad jokes than any other kind of humor.

It's very unfair, because there was a time when you were actually *rewarded* for your bravery. At some point, you asked something like, "Why aren't human beans green?" and everyone laughed and complimented your intelligence.

You were four years old.

Soon, you were intoxicated with the visual puns in *Where's Waldo*, you had a passion for knock-knock jokes,[2] and you were a fan of the *"What were you eating under there?" "Under where?" "You were eating underwear?"* routine. Ooh, here was another good one:

---

**1.** BTW, if you ever want to find Dad jokes in the wild, just walk down any pier and read the boat names.

**2.** "Knock-knock." "Who's there?" "Tank." "Tank who?" "You're welcome! LOL"

**What's brown and sticky?**
**A stick.**

Children love to play with words and make surprising connec-
tions of meaning—and it's adorable. Just this week, I was treated

to seeing a five-year-old crack up at "When Mary took her lambs for haircuts, she went to a baa-baa shop." Kids also like to experiment with unexpected word uses, like that time you said you wanted to eat more pie, but you'd "run out of stomach." And again, everyone laughed and praised your creativity.

But since you're not a kid anymore, the reactions to your wit are different today. And *that's* where your courage comes in. Now, everyone expects you to excuse yourself for still being amazingly creative and funny. It's a complete turnaround of expectations! Let's say you just uttered this joke:

**I was crestfallen after our family's coat of arms crashed to the floor.**

Due to societal expectations, you may be tempted to add an apology such as:

*I'm sorry.*

*I'll see myself out.*

*Goodnight, everyone.*

And the classic:

*No pun intended* (or should I say, No pun inten-*dad*?).

Of course, you don't have to *say* anything. Some Dad jokers just shrug, or throw down a smoke bomb and vanish. (I like to do a bad pop-and-lock and then walk backwards out of the room.) But no matter your style, please remember that the pun is always intended . . . even when it's not.

Your courageous perseverance in the face of zero encouragement makes you one of the special people to know the eventual joy of getting a roomful of people to laugh, or of being fist-bumped by a teenager who's cheering, "Good one!"

I kid. That never happens.

Yet despite the disapproving silences, the anguished groans, the mass unfollowings on Twitter, and the credible threats of violence, you continue in the Dad joking tradition. It's a gift and a curse: You have the perspective to look at something in at least two ways—the way it *is*, and *another* way. Your pun is double-talk that makes your listener do a double-take, and therein lies the joke.

**Did you hear about the multitasking king who ran several kingdoms?**
**He kept a firm hand on the reigns.**

**My wife got me a new lectern for my classroom, but I kept sighing for the good old dais.**

**When Samantha returned home, she found that someone had stolen every lamp in the house. She was absolutely delighted.**

In the following pages, you'll see jokes that may defy what you think of as funny.[3] But not so fast! Sure, some of these jokes may look bad on paper—but when *you* give them life, trust me: they'll be *gold*.

---

**3.** That's my polite way of saying that you might think some of the puns here suck.

# Dad Joke Shout-Out

## BOB'S BURGERS

Each episode of this cartoon features a "Burger of the Day" entry on the restaurant's chalkboard menu. These burgers are usually either Dad joke puns by Bob or more risqué puns from his wife, Louise.[4] Examples of Bob's work include:

**Mushroom With a View Burger (porcini on a double decker)**

**Bleu by You Burger (locally sourced bleu cheese)**

**I Know Why the Cajun Burger Sings**

**Beets of Burden Burger (served with lots of beets)**

**Shoot Out at the Okra Corral Burger**

**Chipotle Off the Old Block Burger**

**The Silentil Night Burger (with lentils)**

**Fifth Day of Christmas Burger (with five golden onion rings)**

**The Final Kraut Down Burger (with sauerkraut)**

---

**4.** "Nothing risqué, nothing gained." —Alexander Woollcott

FREE OF CHARGE!
WAH WAH WAHHHH
FLATLINE
TONY'S DEAD BATTERY City

# Pun IntenDad

*Ed: It's a metaphor.*
*Will: What's a metaphor?!*
*Ed: Mostly sheep and cows to graze in.*
*—Daniel Wallace, Big Fish*

In 1719, Thomas Sheridan wrote a booklet called *The Art of Punning*. It was basically a Dad joke guidebook that included these three rules:

1. You can interrupt any conversation (no matter how serious!) with a pun.

2. You should be the first to laugh at your own joke.

3. If a pun is made, it must be repeated over and over to everyone present until you're sure that everyone definitely heard and got the joke.

This is still fantastic advice, but let's expand on and update these Dad joke guidelines:

4. Ask yourself this question when considering a joke: "Can I imagine a sad trombone sound (*wah-wah-whaa*) or a rim shot (*ba-doom-bah!*) after its punchline?" If yes, make your joke.[1]

Ex. "Today, I gave away my old batteries, free of charge!"

---

**1.** Instead of sound effects, you can substitute in yourself saying "Gotcha!" or asking "Get it? Get it?" or "Did you see what I did there?" and then repeating the joke.

*sad trombone spontaneously plays in background*

5. If you think your audience is in doubt, be sure to explain why your joke was funny. (Actually, you might want to just always do this to save yourself the guesswork.)

6. While some people are sticklers for what is or isn't a pun, in this book, almost any joke that relies on wordplay is defined as a pun.

When prompted by any version of the following questions, you are legally required to respond with the following Dad jokes:

**"Can you make me breakfast?"**
**"Abracadabra, you're breakfast."**

**"Can I watch TV?"**
**"Sure, just don't turn it on."**

**"Hey Dad, can you put my shoes on?"**
**"No, they won't fit me."**

**"I need to change."**
**"But I like you just the way you are!"**

**"Mom, do you know where my sunglasses are?"**
**"No, do you know where my mom glasses are?"**

**"Dad, did you get a haircut?"**
**"No, I got them all cut."**

**"When can I call?"**
**"Call me whenever you want, just don't call me late for dinner."**

You can also initiate these dialogues with your own question:

**"Do your socks have holes in them?"**
**"No."**
**"Then how do you put them on?"**

Now let's look at some of the basic patterns for a Dad joke. They include:

## FAKE-OUT NON-JOKES

Q: What's the difference between Nickelback and a doorknob?
A: Nickelback is a rock group. A doorknob is a device that closes a door.

## "WHEN I WAS YOUR AGE" JOKES

"When I was your age, my dad always fed me alphabet soup. He claimed that I loved it, but he was just putting words in my mouth."

## CORNY PHYSICAL HUMOR

1. Examine someone's coat and ask, "Is that felt?"
2. Then touch the fabric and exclaim, "Now it is!"

## THE "ACTUALLY, YOU MIGHT WANNA RE-THINK THAT" GAGS

These are the truly unfortunate ideas that still get acted upon. For example, I'm sure that running through the zoo's parking lot while screaming, "Run for your lives! They're loose!" *seemed* like a good idea at the time, but . . .

# INTENTIONALLY MISUNDERSTANDING THE OTHER PERSON

During a game of Battleship:

"I-1."

"No way, I still have two ships left."

"Very funny, Dad. I meant that I'm calling an attack on I-1."

"Hang on, I just got a weird text on my phone."

"What is it?"

"A small device used to send and receive information."[2]

"Arg!"

# TWO DAD JOKES TO RULE THEM ALL

There are two Dad Jokes of Power that reign supreme over all others. The first Dad Joke of Power is any variation on this pattern:

**"I'm hungry."**
**"Hi, Hungry, I'm Dad."**

At some point, your child may have heard this routine so many times, they respond with, "Why did you name me Hungry, Dad?" Should this occur, congratulate yourself for being an excellent parent.

---

**2.** To use the dialogue formula from the movie *Airplane!*, this punchline would be "a small device used to send and receive information. But that's not important right now." (Also, this is a classic bit from the Marx Brothers: "Taxes? My uncle's from Taxes." "No, not Texas, taxes. Dollars, taxes!" "That's where he's from! Dollas, Taxes!")

The second Dad Joke of Power is the "Pull my finger" gag. Grandparents are particularly gifted at this joke's execution. If you're ever looking for a fresh twist on this bit, have the kid pull your finger, and then act relieved: "Thank you! My finger has been dislocated for weeks, but you fixed it."

## Great Moments in Dad Joke History

### JAMES JOYCE

This legendary writer's father was from the Irish city of Cork. So James Joyce kept a landscape picture of Cork in his apartment.

The picture was framed in cork.

### IT WAS THE BEST OF PUNS, IT WAS THE WORST OF PUNS

Laughter is a reflex action to a stimulus, like pulling your hand from a flame or extending your hand to a pulled-pork sandwich. But laughter is unique in that it doesn't serve any biological function except to release tension.

**Two antennas got married. The ceremony wasn't much but the reception was excellent.**

What makes a Dad joke unique is that it can both release *and* create tension. (Or create and release tension, depending on how you do it.)

**No, kids, I am not "street smart." But I am crafty in cul-de-sacs.**

**KID: How do I look?**
**DAD: With your eyes.**

What I mean is that for some people, puns always create tension because they think that *any* pun is automatically awful. These misguided folks have bought into the cliché about how the pun is the lowest form of humor.

That's *so* wrong.

Historically, wordplay was often looked upon as the *highest* expression of wit! After all, words are what we use to think. Right now, words are parading in front of you and you are thinking about them. To find humor or a double-meaning for a joke means you have to be able to consider multiple meanings for these words simultaneously. That means you are *thinking about thinking*, which is a meta mental process.[3]

Here are some people who also think about thinking: brain surgeons, comedians, poets, lawyers, psychologists, teachers . . . the cream of the human crop. (Except for the lawyers, anyway.) And you are one of the special people who can plumb the depths of thought and language, dive down in a magical way that scientists can't fathom, and bring up comic treasure. So to make a Dad joke is to revolt against the usual rules of language use. In your own nonthreatening way, you are embracing the outlaw lifestyle.

**My new lifeguard job? I'm drowning in work, and the place I'm at is a real dive. But other than that, it's going swimmingly.**

---

**3.** That's smart-person talk for "hella intelligent."

There are a lot of Dad jokes in this book, and as you go, the jokes will get a little less obvious. That's because the more surprising the jump between a word's literal meaning and a pun, the more likely people will laugh. (It's also more likely that they won't get it, but we'll deal with that later.)

Say you want to make a pun about bread. You immediately think of puns like "raising dough" and "that's how I roll" and "you're good for muffin." And while those are all okay jokes, they're a dime a baker's dozen.

But what about this:

**The Indian restaurant's location was a closely guarded secret. Before I was allowed to eat there, I had to sign a naan-disclosure agreement.**

It's better, right? That's because it has a bigger jump between the word's literal meaning and the pun, so it's more of a surprise. In fact, when I read that pun, I can almost hear a "YEAH!" in the background.

## CSI: DAD JOKES

Any one-liner used in a crime program right before a commercial break is likely to be a Dad joke. In *CSI: Miami*, the actor David Caruso turned this bit into an art form. As Lieutenant Horatio Caine, he'd start a line of dialogue, then put on his sunglasses to make a dramatic Dad joke. This was followed by a howl of "YEAH!" from the Who song "Won't Get Fooled Again."

For example:
*Police Officer*: The perp is missing from the scene. Maybe he took off.

*Lieutenant Horatio Caine*: Or maybe [*puts on sunglasses*], he got taken for a ride.

**"YEAH!"**

*Police Officer*: She came down here to drink some mojitos and catch some sun.

*Lieutenant Horatio Caine*: Well, it looks like something [*puts on sunglasses*] caught *her*.

**"YEAH!"**

With that in mind, please enjoy the following dialogue inspired by David Caruso's character, Lieutenant Horatio Caine:

*Police Officer*: The victim is missing his head.

*Lieutenant*: Then it looks like this case [*puts on sunglasses*] is a no-brainer.

*Officer*: His medical bracelet says he was the recipient of a heart transplant.

*Lieutenant*: So you could say he had [*takes off glasses*] a change of heart.

*Officer*: Hang on, the victim's ID says his name was Buzz.

*Lieutenant*: So it's a real [*puts on glasses*] Buzz kill.

*Officer*: The evidence suggests that the other victim may have been poisoned by flan. The lab tests will show one way or the other.

*Lieutenant*: So the proof [*takes off glasses*] is in the pudding.

*Officer*: Meanwhile, another suspect fled the crime scene at breakneck speed, then ran into a pole and knocked himself out.

*Lieutenant*: Well, he really should've seen [*drops glasses*] that coming.

*Police Captain*: Lieutenant, you are relieved of command.

*Lieutenant*: I guess you could say—

*Police Captain*: Just get out.

**"YEAH!"**

# BE A GOOD AUDIENCE

Kids look up to you. (Look, just pretend, okay?) Since nothing's worse than a bad sport, be sure to role model for kids the proper audience reactions. If someone—*especially* a kid—makes a joke, give them the reaction they want: groaning or laughter, or both.

For example, a girl at a writing festival recently told me this joke:

**Q: When did Anakin Skywalker become evil?**
**A: In the sith grade!**

After she told it, I clapped my hands together, laughed, and thanked her. This wasn't an act—I liked her joke, and I especially liked that she was willing to tell me it. That took courage, so I displayed my appreciation.

Anytime we hear a joke, we generally have one of these three reactions:

*Did I get the joke?*
If so, react in some way. And if you *didn't* get the joke, you can still try to say something nice! The rule is that "not getting a joke" is always the fault of the listener, not the teller. (I don't know if that's actually true, but better to err on the side of kindness.)

*Do I wish I'd thought of that joke?*
If so, be sure to pay the wit a compliment.

*Was that even supposed to be a joke?*

If you're unsure, just ask. But y'know, ask sincerely, not in a snarky way. That way the person who told the joke can explain it to you.

**Important Note:** Some people think that the biggest rule in comedy is "Never Explain the Joke." That's because nothing is more unfunny than an explanation of *why* something is funny. (Just look at this book, for example.)

However!

Dad jokes *should* be explained, often and repeatedly. It doesn't matter if your audience "got it" the first time, repetition can make things funnier. Or more painful. Either way, it's a win for you. And be sure to always preface your remarks with "This is funny because . . . "[4]

**"We're taking on water," the captain announced, then he paused to let the words sink in.**

## SINCERITY VS. IRONY

As I stated earlier: Dad jokes aren't cool, but they *are* awesome. So consider what kind of person you are. Are you someone who sincerely and even innocently loves wordplay and giving people a laugh? Let's call Dad jokes like these "carefree puns."

Or do you want to make a meta comment on comedy by ironically dropping grown-up puns that you know are bad? The writer Wendy Molyneux calls these "sweaty puns."

---

**4.** I do that a lot in this book. Enjoy!

Whether you're sincere or ironic, let's look at the way you should process your Dad joke choices:

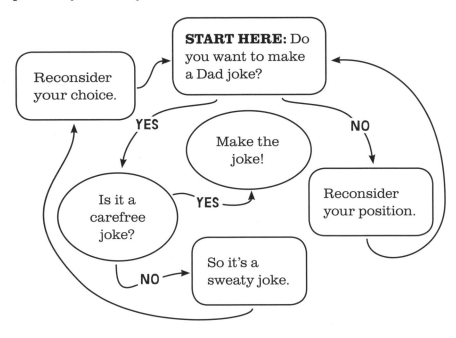

Once, I cut through a field of thistles. I was going through a rough patch.

Why, yes, I do like reading stories about cloistered religious women. In other words, nun fiction.

If I could stop the flow of water with a mild compliment, I'd be damming it with faint praise.

# ORIGINALITY

Up until now, your life has been a voyage from one level of humor to another. So think of this book as a huge step backward.

Of course, many have walked this way before. As I mentioned, at one time, you were a knock-knock joke enthusiast. These jokes have been around so long, there's a knock-knock joke in Shakespeare's *Macbeth*.[5] And if you think about it, all archery humor consists of "nock nock" jokes.

**While William Tell was the most famous archer in history, both he and his family members were also avid bowlers. But since all league records are lost, we'll never know for whom the Tells bowled.[6]**

I'm guessing you don't tell a lot of knock-knock jokes anymore, because at some point, you realized, "Been there, punned that." Fair enough, but remember, repetition is an important part of our art form. There are theoretically a finite number of ways that words can be combined and interpreted. Which is to say that there are billions of puns available to us, but that's not an infinite amount.

So in some cases, a Dad joker recycles old bits. And even if you "discover" or "invent" a pun, the odds are good that your particular pun has been done before. You're just sort of re-excavating it.

---

**5.** Act II, Scene 3.

**6.** This is funny because it's a takeoff on the title of Ernest Hemingway's novel, *For Whom the Bells Tolls*.

**As I studied the Chinese finger trap encasing my digits, I realized I had a real mystery on my hands.**

But don't let that put you off. My attitude is that if it's the first time *I've* thought of a pun, then it counts as a new one for me. Speaking of which, this book's puns come from three general sources. Hoary, old, and moss-covered puns are one source. Another are specific jokes credited to specific people. And finally, there are the jokes that I've come up with on my own. I didn't go through and label each one because that would be annoying, and I'm pushing the envelope of annoyingness as it is. And speaking of annoying, let me now present . . .

## *THE CASE OF THE PURLOINED PUN*

Let me set the scene: A group of people—perhaps family or co-workers—are chatting about an silly, fun topic, e.g. what it would be like to be invisible.

*You (deadpan)*: Let me be perfectly clear, being invisible would be fun. [*silence*]

*Todd*: Let you be perfectly *clear*? CLEAR? [*makes "ta-dah" motion; everyone laughs*]

*You (feeling betrayed)*: I see what you did there. You poached my joke.

*Todd*: Well, I couldn't tell if you were trying to be funny or if it was just an accident.

*You*: But you literally took the words right out of my mouth.

*Todd*: Wow, I'm being accused of joke stealing? I did not *see* that coming! [*laughter*]

*You (trying to be a good sport)*: I'm just aiming for maximum transparency. [*silence*]

*Todd*: You're aiming for *maximum transparency*? [*more laughter*] Get it?

*You*: Yes, I get it! I just said it!

*Everyone*: [*rolling their eyes*]

If there's a lesson to be learned from the Case of the Purloined Pun, it's that it is almost impossible to regain ownership of a joke once someone else takes it. This sort of pun-sploitation is vastly unfair, and it's why we should be good role models and credit jokes back to their sources whenever possible.

Unless they're mine; you can go ahead and use those. (Wait, you paid for this book, right?)

## Know Your Dad Joke

## THE HEAD FAKE

Want to seem clever? Who doesn't? So during conversations, try randomly dropping a "No pun intended" into the thread every now and then. This will make people listen to you more carefully, as they try to figure out what genius-level jokes you're uttering that they're missing out on.

But the punchline is that *there aren't any puns at all*.

# Mala-Pops

**Dick Smothers: Did you go to the wedding?**
**Tommy Smothers: Yes, and I went to the conception afterwards.**
**Dick: You mean reception.**
**Tommy: I must've been in the wrong room.**

A *malaprop* is what happens when someone uses a similar-sounding but incorrect word for an idiom, phrase, synonym, name, or just about any other type of word. Yet while a prop comic is scorned by other comedians, a malaprop can make an interesting Dad joke.

**The Grand Canyon sure is gorges.**

**Pastafarians conclude their prayers with the word, "Ramen". (And the Church of the Flying Spaghetti Monster has a crèche called "Touched by an Angelhair.")**

**"Why are you pulling vegetation out of that lovely stream?"**
**"I'm weeding a good brook."**

My dad specialized in malaprops, and he drove us kids bonkers by saying certain words and phrases incorrectly. At one point he convinced me that "sawhorse" is the past tense of "seahorse." And like many parents, he also took a strange pleasure in embarrassing and aggravating us by mispronouncing words, or simply using the *wrong* words. And he'd never learn from his mistakes! No matter how many times we corrected his usage, Dad would use it wrong the next time.

**"I can't remember; guess I have anemia."**
**"For the last time, it's *amnesia*."**
**"What'd I say?"**
**"Anemia!"**
**"That's what I just said: Anemia."**

Etc.

This trolling extended to nicknames. Dad nicknamed everyone, and would then profess ignorance if you used that person's *actual* name. For example, he called my sister Melinda "Boom."

**"So Melinda was telling me—"**
**"Who?"**
**"Your daughter, Melinda."**
**"I don't know who you're talking about."**
***sigh* "Boom."**
**"Oh, Boom, of course! What about her?"**

Over the course of time, I eventually realized Dad was trolling us. Yes, he knew the difference between *prostate* and *prostrate*, but he was engaging in malaprop warfare. For his own nefarious reasons, he loved hearing us scoff and groan. And of course our attempts to correct him never worked, because when it comes to malaprops, the pie's the limit.

But why would he do this? The German word *schadenfreude* is defined as "pleasure derived by someone from another person's misfortune." Perhaps there is a parental version of it called

29

*dad-enfreude*: The loving glee that a parent derives from inflicting questionable jokes upon their children.[1]

It's also been suggested Dad jokes may have been my father's harmless payback for the frustrations that we children inflicted on him. Ha! What a laugh. Unless I have anemia, we were all perfect children who were a constant delight.

**In second grade, I had to sit in the corner alone for misbehavior. But that was an isolated incident.**

**When I hear thunder, grape vines always reassure me. (There's nothing like a safe arbor in a storm.)**

## Know Your Dad Joke

### ACCENT DEPUN-DENT

These are Dad jokes that depend on accents and local pronunciations. For example, this one from Boston:

**A real estate agent tells a client that the house they're about to see doesn't have a flaw. "No flaw?" asks the client. "What d'ya walk on?"**

### TEXAS:

**So this cowboy walks into a German car showroom and says, "Audi." (By Tim Vine)**

---

**1.** I have a friend whose father didn't like to "let any moment pass unimproved." This is also a great justification for using dad jokes—they just make life better!

*CANADA:*

The new superhero, Maple Leaf Woman, fights for . . .

## IRELAND:

A wee boy goes into a cake shop, points in the window and asks, "Is that a cake or a meringue?" "No, you're right," says the baker. "It's a cake."

An Irish grandfather is teaching his grandson a recipe for bean soup. He tells the boy to add exactly 239 beans. "But why, Grandpa?" the lad asks. The grandfather answers, "Because if you add just one more bean, it'll be too farty."

## AUSTRALIA:

A man traveling in the outback takes a bad fall off a cliff, and awakens to find himself in the house of a rancher. "Was I brought here to die?" asks the man. "No, mate," replies the rancher, "you were brought here yester-die."

Finally, here is a venerable and time-honored[2] accent-dependent joke: "You know the difference between a stoic and a cynic? A stoic is what brings the babies, and a cynic is what you wash them in."

"I see there's a photo of me in your locket."
"Yes. I want you to be in-de-pendant."

---

**2.** Also known as a "moldy oldy."

# Timing for the Perfect Groan

## "The pun is the guano of the winged mind."
### —Victor Hugo, Les Misérables

Victor Hugo may have poo-pooed puns, but he also loved making them in person. There's a good chance that the writer enjoyed seeing the expressions on the faces of his ~~victims~~ audience as his jokes landed. Yet, try as I might, the puns in this book can't land with the same force as they would out in the real world. That's because there is a certain magic in coming up with a perfect joke spontaneously and in the moment. That's why I sometimes try to set a stage here by using dialogue.

### "Hey, how was that mime class you took?"
### "Unspeakable."

Some Dad jokes work well, some barely work, and some just *don't*. For example, if I said, "Little Timmy isn't spoiled rotten, he's spoiled *fresh*," even a Dad joker would look away with pity on their face.

Why? True, that joke's not clever, but people groan at bad puns all the time. But the wordplay doesn't even make sense; there's just something anti-humorous and non-Dad jokey there. It's not corny, it's just wrong. My wife, Lynn, calls these jokes TTH:

Trying Too Hard. There's too much of a stretch, and the effort shows.

## SELF CONTROL

Being able to recognize a TTH joke can help fend off your worst impulses. For example, I've noticed that the word "chemotherapy" has "mother" inside of it. But try as I might, there just doesn't seem to be any way to convert that information into a good bad joke. I am also convinced that there is a way to make an Edgar Allan Poe Dad joke using, "Quoth the Raven 'Demi Moore.'" But how?

For the moment, I must be patient.

This book has *lots* of Dad jokes, but they're just going to sit there on the page until you breathe life into them. By using the following techniques, I can ensure that you get a response of *some* kind.[1]

**Bumping into a friend who's an elderly tailor:
"Why, you old sew-and-sew!"**

## TIMING AND DELIVERY

"Hard-boiled eggs aren't all they're cracked up to be" is a joke that's been shelled out many times before. So for maximum effectiveness, use it with a set-up. For example, at some point, you'll be in a position where you can ask a kid, "Hey, do you like hard-boiled eggs?"

---

**1.** *evil laugh*

Their response doesn't matter—because whatever they say, wait a beat, then reply, "They're not all they're cracked up to be."

You just imagined the sad trombone sound, right? Good job. So set up your Dad jokes when you can. That audience participation will increase your listener's enjoyment.

But what kind of *style* should you use when delivering that line? Depending on your mood and your audience's age and maturity level, you have a full spectrum of joke delivery systems available to you.

## JOKE DELIVERY OPTIONS

### FULL HAM

Text: There is no such thing as over-acting, because you're selling this joke as hard as you can.

Best For: Small children, people who unconditionally love you

Role Models: William Shatner, Lucy Lawless, overly-caffeinated improv comedians

### HALF HAM

Text: You have a merry gleam in your eye as you set up your joke. You're working it, but holding a little something back.

Best for: Centrists, situations where you're unsure of which way to lean

Role Models: Ali Wong, Jerry Seinfeld, Hannibal Buress

### DEADPAN

Text: You deliver the joke the same way you'd say, "I need to tie my shoelaces."[2]

Best for: Teens, government officials

Role Models: Aubrey Plaza, Steven Wright

**If troops were told how to pass small marsupials from soldier to soldier, they'd be trained in hand-to-hand wombat.**

**My parents thought it'd be a good idea for my brother and I to stack our beds. This notion was quickly debunked.**

## HAVE FUN

Steve Martin's early stand-up comedy depended on him *pretending* that he thought his material was absolutely hilarious. (It was actually very silly.) So no matter what your delivery style

---

2. A person who doesn't speak English wouldn't know that you just told a joke.

is, the key to telling your Dad joke is that you must seem to be *enjoying yourself.*

**I put myself through college by working in an adhesives factory. (That's my story, and I'm sticking to it.)**

That joke you just told is a delight! It's your enjoyment that will drive your audiences berserk with love and rage.

**The ghost in the bathroom noted that the houseguest had done something unpleasant. It tried to press the toilet's handle, but while the spirit was willing, the flush was weak.**

**I just saw my Grandpa with a young, tattooed bearded guy wearing red pants.**
**So I asked, "Who is that?" and my Grandpa said, "My hip replacement."**

A clever Dad joke doesn't need to be laughed at to elicit admiration. (This is what I tell myself, anyway.) A really great one might elicit heartfelt groans. Outraged cries of betrayal, silent, tight-lipped agony, and the symptoms of nausea are also terrific. The key is getting a *reaction.*

To understand what I'm getting at, consider this: The average TV sitcom operates on the "70 percent rule." The idea is that 70 percent of the audience should get any given joke and hopefully laugh. But for people like us, ratios like these are useless. You're playing by different rules entirely, and so our expectations should shift. What we need for gauging audience reactions is:

# THE DAD JOKE SCORING CHART

| Audience Reaction | What's Happening | Score |
|---|---|---|
| No reaction, life continues uninterrupted | They didn't hear you; repeat the joke louder! | *0* |
| A deadpan expression that says, "I will cut you" | Person heard but refuses to let you break their will to live | *1* |
| Listener says "ba-dum-ching" or shrugs with their face | This is the bare minimum acceptable response | *2* |
| Audible exhaled snort; scattered boos | Now we're getting somewhere | *3* |
| Any fake laugh (e.g. "Har-dee-har-har") or sarcastic comment ("Good one") | Keep at it, you'll wear them down | *4* |
| Grim silence and tight-lipped agony | They want to complain, but fear encouraging you | *5* |
| Listener simply repeats the pun with a headshake | This is a good sign | *6* |
| A muttered oath; someone yells, "Delete your account!" | Your parents are proud of you | *6.5* |
| A grudging affirmation/tip of the hat: "That was actually pretty good" | Your body releases dopamine | *7* |
| Dead silence where you can hear a pun drop; audience avoids eye contact | Your heartbeat speeds up and your pupils dilate | *7.5* |
| Loud groans, disgusted exclamations of "Da-ad! Geez." | Add two bonus points if you're not their dad | *8* |
| Outraged cries of betrayal, credible threats of violence | Your humor stirs passions; keep stirring | *8.5* |
| Legitimate laughter | You get goosebumps | *9* |
| Uncontrollable laughter | Now you're giving *me* goosebumps! | *10* |

# EXPRESSIONS OF REMORSE

After your joke's made, you may choose to flee the scene of the crime. But if you decide to stick around, remind your audience that there are proven social and health benefits to sharing humor. (This is true, BTW.) And if they want to know what those benefits are, say, "The look on your face just now."

But depending on whether or not you have a conscience, your jokes may fill you with real or imaginary grief. Don't worry, this is normal, more's the pity. In some cases, it can add comedic effect to your joke if you express that grief shortly afterwards. You can pretend your joke was an unhappy accident or go with the time-honored phrase "pardon the pun" (which dates back at least to the eighteenth century). There are also handy modern expressions like:

*I am very sorry.*
*I'll see myself out.*
*Haha, oh god, kill me now.*
*A thousand apologies to you and your family.*
*Mea culpa, mea culpa, mea maxima culpa.*

## Dad Joke Hall of Fame

## PAULIE WALNUTS

After Paulie Walnuts of *The Sopranos* tells a joke, he chuckles and asks, "Did you hear what I said?"

Then he repeats the *exact same joke*.

*chef's kiss*

# CORPSING

If you ever hit a ten on the Dad Joke Scoring Chart, rest assured that your name will go down in history. Because you've gotten your audience to do something only a select few people have ever accomplished: corpsing, or "cracking up so hard that they break character." It's a term started by actors who were supposed to be playing dead bodies onstage, aka "corpses." For some totally illogical reason, those actors who were *supposed* to hold still and look dead would sometimes giggle and then get hysterical with laughter.

While there is no way to predict what will make someone corpse, people do tend to laugh along with someone else, even if they have no idea what that person is laughing about. But while everyone might laugh the first, second, or even third time someone corpses, after that, they just get annoyed.

**I was startled to see that my rap battle opponent brought extensive notes with him. I mean, his rap sheet was as long as my arm.**

**That angry robot is mad as HAL.**

**My carefully stacked logs fell over in a pile in what I'm assuming was a timber tantrum.**

Strangely, having everyone else get annoyed does not usually help the corpsing actor *stop* laughing. In fact, it can make the problem get worse. If you've ever gotten hysterical when nobody else was laughing and everyone else was looking at you with a mixture of disgust and wonder, you know what I mean.

But if you can make someone else corpse? That's a Very Good Thing. The fact is that people are goofy and it's hard to know exactly what they'll laugh at, so well done.[3] A British comedy

---

**3.** In the original *The Wizard of Oz* movie, there is a scene where Judy Garland (who plays Dorothy) slaps the Cowardly Lion. The Lion then cries in a funny way. If you watch Dorothy in the scene, she starts smiling and almost cracks up.

show called *The Goodies* ran a skit where a Scottish man in a kilt used his bagpipes to defend himself from a giant pudding. One viewer laughed so hard at this, he fell over, stone dead. Was this a tragedy? Maybe! But the gentleman's wife sent a very nice letter to the staff at TV program, thanking them for giving her husband such a pleasant send-off.

**I like landscapers because they're easy to get a lawn with.**

If you think of the times when *you've* laughed hysterically, odds are high that it was a "you had to be there" moment that would be hard to explain to a rational person. The lesson here is that there is always a chance that *your* dumb Dad joke that barely makes sense just may hit someone right on the funny bone and make them corpse.

In a good way.

**Is this hit man up to snuff?**

**You can do your geometry homework, if you are so inclined.**

**"I see your point."**
**—Me, after being stabbed through the back by a swordsman.**

## Know Your Dad Joke

### HOMOPHONIC PUNS ALOUD

A homophone is a word that can be confused with a different word because of how it's pronounced. Like "aloud" and "allowed" or "ate" and "eight." They can also be a bit more of a stretch, like if your friend warned you about her son:

**He's incorrigible, so please do not incorrige him.**

Or maybe someone in the music business told you:

**I have a Slovakian friend who makes microphones.
And a Czech one, too. A Czech one, too.**

A homophonic pun make us stop and think for a moment. Like if you ask someone how their vacation to Southeast Asia was, and they said, "Great! I had a Laos-y time."

Languages, like English, Yiddish, Hebrew, Japanese, and Chinese are blessed with *lots* of homophones.[4] But homophonic puns can be especially tricky when they happen *across* languages. For example, here's a sophisti-cat-ed bilingual kids' riddle:

**An American cat and a French cat agreed to race in the swimming pool. The American cat was named One-Two-Three. The French cat was named Un-Deux-Trois. Who won the race?**
**Answer: The American cat wins, because the Un-Deux-Trois cat sank.[5]**

While these jokes work better when said aloud, then again, so do many non-homophonic Dad jokes, like:

**Once you've seen one giant shopping center, you've seen 'em all.
I'd tell you some tax jokes, but I doubt you'd depreciate it.**

---

**4.** I encourage you to look at the amaze-balls Wikipedia page, "Homophonic Puns in Mandarin Chinese."
**5.** This is funny because un, deux, trois, quatre, cinq = 1, 2, 3, 4, 5 in French. And "quatre" and "cinq" are pronounced like "cat" and "sank." Voila!

**Do you know what propaganda is?**
**Yes, it's when a British person takes a good look at something.**

You know how Charlie Brown always gets rocks for treats at Halloween? As a kid, I loved it when a *Peanuts* cartoon had students getting assigned countries for geography and Charlie Brown said, "I got Iraq." Oh, and here's a riddle-verse from

Richard Whately (1787–1863) that qualifies as something that's funnier when said out loud:

**Why can't you starve in the desert?**
**Because of the sand which is there.**
**Who brought the sandwiches there?**
**Noah sent Ham, and his descendants mustered and bred.**

**A slice of coconut pie is $3.50 in Jamaica and $4.00 in the Bahamas. These are the pie rates of the Caribbean.**

Yet just as some Dad jokes are better heard not seen, others only really work visually. For example, this excerpt from a play's script:

**[stage left]**
**Macbeth: Where's the stage gone?**

This might be a good time to mention these other two pun flavors which are sometimes confused with homophonic puns:

**Homographic pun:** two words with the same spelling, but different meanings and often different sounds, e.g. "wound": an injury OR to wrap something.

**Homonymic puns:** Words with two meanings that are spelled *and* sound the same, like "belt" (the noun around your pants) and "belt" (the way a singer projects their voice).

# Music

## "Then I CC'd every girl that I see-see 'round town." —Andre 3000

Good news, everyone! I just dropped my new album. Now just give me a moment to sweep up all these broken LP fragments on the floor.

Okay, where was I? Oh yeah, music. There are so many clever lyricists and erudite rappers who are Dad jokers in disguise, keeping track of their wordplay would take an entire book of its own. I mean, where would I even start? With this line, from Jarvis Cocker of the band Blur?

**"I met her in the museum of paleontology/And I make no bones about it."**

Or this, from the BNL?

**"If I had a million dollars
Well, I'd buy you some art
A Picasso or a Garfunkel."[1]**

Look, these artists are decidedly clever, but I am not. To support that statement, let me point out that the Beatles have a pun-based name. You know, b-e-a-t.

---

**1.** This is funny because Art Garfunkel is a person. (And as for that BNL, what, you think I'm just going to write "Bare Naked Ladies" in a family-friendly book? Wrong.)

*Beat*les.

It's a punny name.

I was twenty-five years old before I noticed this.

**"Is that some kind of a mitten on your hand?"**
**"No, it's a crazy little thing called glove."**

And I was even older when someone asked if I'd heard the album from a group called Brand X called *Moroccan Roll.*

"Morocco," I thought, looking for an angle. "Is that like 'Marrakesh Express' or something? Is it a vacation destination? A counterculture reference?"

Later, I realized that the title was just a reference to "More Rock and Roll." Duh. I was so lousy at spotting this kind of humor, I felt like throwing a tantrum. And why not? I'm old and dramatic, so I qualify as a "pre-Madonna prima donna."

## *YEAH!*

But musicians are so cool, they get away with using Dad jokes with their reputations intact. I mean, think about U2's name.[2] It's barely a Dad joke at all. Horace Panter, the bass player for the fast-paced reggae group the Specials, wrote a book called *Ska'd for Life*. And the famous Irish group the Cranberries were originally called the Cranberry Saw Us. Get it? "The cranberry sauce."

Before being the guitar player for Sleater-Kinney, Carrie Brownstein ran for office at her elementary school. Her slogan

---

**2.** Pro Bono is a guy who works for the band.

was, "We built this city on rock 'n' roll, but we should build this *school* upon leadership." (She won.)

Greg and Duane Allman founded the Allman Brothers, but prior to that, they were in a band called the Allman Joys. (Really.)

That food-related pun reminds me that I'm writing a stage musical set in colonial America. It's about a community's food poisoning epidemic from bad pork. The play is called *Ham-ill-town*. (Also, it might be true that I once played percussion for an arty emo band called Rimbaud. I wasn't very good, so I was there mostly for the cymbalism.)

Few people know that Jim Morrison and a young Ric Ocasek almost formed a rock group that was going to be called the Car Doors.

When bands are extremely successful, they spawn their own tribute bands. For example, the Grateful Dead inspired the Grateful Shred. Roxy Music has Proxy Music. Nirvana has Nearvana. Loverboy has Coverboy. Oasis has both No Way Sis and Oasish. And I love that Creedence Clearwater Revival has Creedence Clearwater Revival Revival.

But my favorite tribute band source is Abba, which has Swede Dreamz, Bjorn Again, *and* Abbadabbadoo. (And while it's unrelated to cover bands, I am very happy to report that there's a Wu-Tang Clan documentary called "Of Mics and Men.")

Classical music is a different genre, yet I should mention that when Arturo Toscanini conducted his first "all-Bach" concert, he pushed his orchestra so relentlessly in rehearsals, they nicknamed him the "Bach Suite Driver."[3] So, bravo, classical musicians. But for now, I'm going to stick with relatively contemporary music, where the artists know how to lay down a good album title:

**Big Daddy Kane:** *Long Live the Kane*
**(The pun: "Long live the king.")**

**Supergrass:** *Road to Rouen*

**Nick Cave and the Bad Seeds:** *From Her to Eternity*

**Go-Go's:** *Beauty and the Beat* [4]

**David Bowie:** *Aladdin Sane*

**Salt-N-Pepa:** *A Salt With A Deadly Pepa*

**Frank Zappa:** *Sheik Yerbouti*

**Alkaline Trio:** *From Here to Infirmary*

**Snoop Dogg:** *Tha Doggfather*

**REO Speedwagon:** *You Can Tune a Piano, But You Can't Tuna Fish*

**Slade:** *Till Deaf Do Us Part*

**Block:** *Lead Me Not into Penn Station*

**Beastie Boys:** *Licensed to Ill*

---

**3.** Also, a study found that movie villains and murderers tend to listen to a disproportionate amount of classical music. (Seriously.) So you could say they're Bach-stabbers.

**4.** What was the name of that Go-Go's song about recuperating from cold sores? Oh yeah—"My Lips Are Healed."

Lorde: *Pure Heroine*

Ian Gomm: *Gomm with the Wind*

Greg Kihn: *Next of Kihn, RocKihnRoll, Kihntinued, Kihnspiracy, Kihntageous, Citizen Kihn,* and *KihnSolidation: The Best of Greg Kihn*

## SONG TITLES

Obviously, there are even more good candidates for Dad joke songs. So let me narrow things down by eliminating Pat Benatar's tribute to a guy who sneezed without covering his mouth, "Hit Me With Your Wet Snot." (It's an easy disqualification since the song doesn't actually exist.)

Now then, the envelopes, please.

There is a tie for the bronze medal between "Looking Out My Window Through the Pain" by Mel Street and "You Can't Have Your Kate and Edith Too" from the Statler Brothers.

The silver medal goes to "Romeo and Oubliette"[5] by Tendon Levey.

And the gold medal goes to the composer Michael Giacchino. He has a song on the *Dawn of the Planet of the Apes* soundtrack called "Monkey See, Monkey Coup." (Giacchino has many other fine examples of the form, including "Here Today, Gone to Maui" from the *Lost* soundtrack.)

---

**5.** An oubliette (oob-lee-ett) is a secret dungeon that can only be accessed via trapdoor.

# MONDEGREENS

I once thought that the Bob Denver hit "Annie's Song" included the line "You fill out my census." This raised many questions for me. Like, why was Annie filling out John Denver's census? Was it a testament to her math skills? Or was she just a rebel who likes filling out other people's forms?

Later, I learned that the line is actually "you fill up my *senses*." Oops. I had committed a mondegreen, which is what happens when you mishear the lyrics to a song. Kids often make the best mondegreens, and one of my kid favorites is:

**"Ring around the rosies
Popsicle emojis"**

And I'll never forget the episode of *Rugrats* where Angelica began singing "America the Beautiful" with "O beautiful, for spaceship eyes . . ." Another time, she mondegreened "My Country, 'Tis of Thee" like this:

**"My country tears of thee
Sweet land of lizardy, of thee I see
Land that my father buyed,
Land of my chill and pie,
From every mountain slide,
Let freedom ring."**

"Okay," you're thinking, "so mondegreens are accidental plays on words. But how are they *Dad jokes*?"

I'm glad you asked! As you know, one of life's greatest rewards is trolling your children. So pick a song your kids are familiar with, and come up with an "accidental" mondegreen of one of its lyrics. Then loudly sing *your* version of the song every time it plays. Or just light into it on your own: in the shower, when you're picking up the kids from school, or when you're tucking them into bed at night. Ignore their agonized wails of protest; they'll love you all the more for this.

A wonderful thing about mondegreens is that listeners sometimes like the wrong version better. Even songwriters can fall victim to their charms. John Fogerty wrote the song "Bad Moon Rising" with the line "there's a bad moon on the rise." Yet in concert, he's been known to perform its common mondegreen: "There's a bathroom on the right."

Here are a few personal mondegreen examples: Elton John's "Rocket Man" has a chorus of: "Rocket man burning out his fuse up here alone..." But as a kid, I heard that as:

**"Rocket man, burning up this room with provolone . . . "**

Elton John also covered this Beatles song:

*"The girl with kaleidoscope eyes*
*Lucy in the sky with diamonds . . ."*

Which I heard as:
**"The girl with colitis goes by**
**Lucy's in a fight with Linus . . ."**

Here's a short list of some other classic rock mondegreens:

"Come together, right now . . . hold the meat" (from the Beatles' "Come Together")

"Juice box hero" (from Foreigner's "Juke Box Hero")

"Bring me an iron lung" (from Steve Winwood's "Bring Me a Higher Love")

"See that girl, watch her scream, kickin' the dancing queen" (from Abba's "Dancing Queen")

"I ransom far away" (from A Flock of Seagulls' "I Ran")

"I'll never leave your pizza burning" (from the Rolling Stones' "Beast of Burden")

"I'm just a pool boy, nobody loves me. He's just a pool boy, from a pool family" (from Queen's "Bohemian Rhapsody")

"If you like bean enchiladas, and getting caught in the rain" (from Rupert Holmes's "Escape (The Piña Colada Song)")

Finally, allow me to share a classic rock pun to end the chapter:

"Hey, this cream-colored bucket is too dark."
"Oh, so you want a lighter shade of pail?"[6]

---

**6.** This is funny because a classic rock album is Procol Harum's *A Whiter Shade of Pale.*

# Dad Joke Shout-Out

## EVIL DEAD II

There is a scene in this fine film where the main character, Ash, has to trap his own disembodied hand under a bucket. Then Ash puts a stack of books on top of the bucket so that his hand can't escape. The top book on that stack: *A Farewell to Arms*.

I'm just now beginning to grasp how awesome that joke is.[7]

**"Let's take a quick recess," said the elementary school teacher, banging a gavel while the class ran for the door.**

---

**7.** Also, Jaime Lannister is singlehandedly my favorite character in *Game of Thrones*.

# Proper Names

*"You have a daughter, I believe?"*
*"Yeah. Yeah, Henrietta."*
*"Did he, did he, I'm sorry to hear that."*
*—Stephen Fry and Hugh Laurie,*
*A Bit of Fry and Laurie*

I used to think jokes that rely on a name to be funny were cheap. So what changed for me? I went to the dog park. There I was, carefully watching my beloved hellhound Augie.[1] And that was when a dog owner near me called out:

**"Come here, Yips! Good dog!"**
**"Your dog's named Yips?" I asked.**
**"Yes," the dog owner said sunnily. "Yips Ahoy."**

Oh. My. GOD.

I saw the light. Of course puns on names are a good thing! True, there are so many obvious names for dogs that Dorothy Parker named *her* dog Cliché. (And if I have to meet another golden retriever named Bailey, I'm going to bail . . . permanently.)

I've learned about dogs named Beowoof, Drools Verne, Harry Paw-ter, Prince of Barkness, Pup the Magic Dragon, Doggie Houndser, Puppy Longstocking, MacArthur Bark, Mary

---

**1.** When he eats certain meats, Augie gets agitated and becomes a flight risk. That day, he was on the lamb.

Puppins, Raise the Woof, The Puppymaster, Collieflower, Barkimaeus, Dunepuppy, Arfie Bunker, and Peter Barker.

Not to mention *Droolius Caesar*.

\*swoon\*

# Great Moments in Dad Joke History

## ROBERT LOUIS STEVENSON

Stevenson's classic novel *The Strange Case of Dr. Jekyll and Mr. Hyde* contains this proper name gem:

"If he be Mr. Hyde . . . I shall be Mr. Seek."

So I've changed my attitude about names and jokes. In fact, just last night, I watched the 1944 film *Laura* and was struck by how good the actress Gene Tierney was.

But I don't know why I was surprised—after all, she had the power of a Tierney.

And I look more fondly upon the *Inspector Gadget* movie with this dialogue:

**DR. CLAW:** I deserve a dashing appellation.
**KRAMER:** "Dashing Appalachian"? What is that, a hillbilly with a tuxedo?
**DR. CLAW:** No, you idiot! It's a nickname.

I also appreciate that when the Beatles' original drummer, Pete Best, came out with his own solo album, he called it *Best of the Beatles*. (This was both diabolically clever and a total rip-off.)

This is not to mention what writer Max Beerbohm said after deciding not to hike up a Swiss Alp with his companions:

**"Put me down as an anti-climb Max."**

Yes, Mr. Beerbohm used his *own* name for a pun. That said, I'm emboldened to offer this story, which is about one of my first efforts at a Dad joke. I was in second grade when the brainstorm for the joke hit me. I didn't know what to do—should I blurt out my joke to the first person who came along?

No! This was too precious for that. Instead, I carried my joke home, where I told my parents the following:

"Um, today for a field trip, Mrs. Pirtle took us downtown. When nobody was watching, I walked into a bar. There was a really mean guy there, and he told me to get out or he'd kill me. Get it? Get it?"

I started laughing, and my parents probably wondered if I had a brain fever. "Because he was a Bart-ender. Get it? A *Bart*-ender!"

Since I was now in hysterics, my memory of their reaction is lost to time. But let's assume it was favorable. Anyway, a few years later, I landed a big (and to date, only) part in a school play. During a rehearsal, the spotlight focused on me—then vanished as my "friend" covered the bulb.

Yes, it was a total eclipse of the Bart.[2]

---

**2.** That's funny because it's a spin on the song "Total Eclipse of the Heart."

# *Know Your Dad Joke*

## APTONYMS

*Aptonyms* are names that are *so* perfect for their owners, they become real-life puns. Think of the sprinter Usain Bolt, or the meteorologists Amy Freeze or Sara Blizzard. My research also revealed that there's a urologist named Alexander Philpott, which is when I stopped researching.

Humorist Gene Weingarten of the *Washington Post* also coined the term *inaptonym*, a name that is so wrong, it seems like a joke, like the pitcher Grant Balfour, or the former Khmer Rouge spokesperson Am Rong.[3]

**"Michael Caine's snubbed me for the last time," I vowed, as the wrecking ball crashed into the actor's mansion. "Now, I am razing Caine."**

**At the bookshop:**
**"OMG, I just saw Judy Blume in one of the book rows!"**
**"Is she still there?"**
**"No, the Blume is off the rows."**

**Jamie Farr (of M\*A\*S\*H) has a memoir titled *Just Farr Fun***

**"Welcome to my midlife Chrysler." —David Gates**

**The novelist John le Carré has a poster in his office that reads "Keep Calm and le Carré On."**

---

**3.** Fun Fact: A major component of your teeth is a phosphate mineral called apatite.

# FIRE AT WILL!

A Greek classics professor goes to a tailor to get his pants mended. The tailor asks him: "Euripides?"
The professor replies: "Yes. Eumenides?"[4]

"I'm going from bad to Hearst." —Journalist William L. Shirer, on going from the *Chicago Tribune* to working for William Randolph Hearst.

(BTW, if I ever have to stand in front of a firing squad, I don't want to be riddled by bullets. I'd prefer a pop quiz.)

---

**4.** It's funny because Euripides was an Athenian playwright in 400 BCE. "The Eumenides" was the third part of a Greek tragedy by Aeschylus. So when it sounds like the tailor asks, "You ripped these?" the professor says, "Yes. You mend these?"

# Know Your Dad Joke

## MANGA EYE ROLLS

At some point, your child may go through a manga phase. If so, fantastic! These Japanese comics are printed right to left, instead of left to right. So be sure to pick up a manga book in front of your child and look at it disbelievingly.

Then cry out:

"How dumb. They printed this book backwards!"

The subsequent "Da-ad!" and eye roll you'll get for being clueless will be like money in your Dad joke bank.

**It doesn't make sense for the FAA to have ground rules for drones. What good is that when they're up in the air?**

**[A crowd gathers at the boathouse.]**
**"Looks like they're announcing who made the rowing team."**
**"Ah, so it's time for a 'crew cut'?"**
**\*splash\***

**If someone disagrees with me, I stick my fingers in my ears, so whatever they say is a mute point.**

# The Miracle of Dad Humor

*"The test of a first-rate intelligence is the ability to hold two opposed ideas in the mind at the same time, and still retain the ability to function." —F. Scott Fitzgerald*

## WHAT HAPPENS IN THE BRAIN

You are brilliant. I'm not just kissing up (or down, depending on your height). I have proof! Glance at the very clever illustration to the right.

As you look at this image, you instantly shuffle through all the possible meanings of the sign's words and the image. Then your brain takes that information and compares it to the illustration.

Translating from words to visuals takes you just a nanosecond, and—

## BAM!

You got the Dad joke. This process happened incredibly quickly. You're so good at this instant interpretation, you can sometimes spot puns coming in a conversation before someone says them.

### A judge who's in a hurry just goes through the motions.

To understand even the simplest pun, you have to simultaneously hold in your mind at least *two* meanings for a word or statement. As you do, you're taking note of what's happening between the spelling of the pun and/or its sound and/or its actual meaning. There's a spark between brain cells, a synthesis of ideas, a creative jump.

That kind of freewheeling intelligence is higher-order thinking, yo. And that was just to *understand* a pun. Imagine what kind of brain activity a pun-trepreneur gets when they *make* a joke.

### Last night, a rancher went on a marathon sleepwalk. Luckily, he came to his fences.

The only way to spot the "rhyming ideas" of a pun is through frontal lobe multitasking, and that's a pretty incredible feat. It's why people who pun have been found to have similar brain activity to freestyling rappers and improvising jazz musicians.

Put it this way: There are twenty-six letters in the alphabet. Everything you've ever read or *could* read in English is just some combination of those letters. As you read this book, you are seeing a letter sequence you've never seen before, and your brain is taking stock, making sense, and finding humor (if

64

I'm lucky) in some of them. The possible variety of sentences, thoughts, and ideas those twenty-six letters can create is seemingly infinite, and as close to a miracle as anything I can imagine.

Aristotle had a word for the ability to quickly spot patterns and make mental jumps: *eutrapelia*. But even if you didn't have a good measure of *eutrapelia*, people would still think you are clever because of this amazing reason: There are a limited amount of *sounds* that the human mouth can make, yet spoken language offers a really complex number of meanings that can be expressed through them. That makes puns unavoidable as you speak, whether you are trying to make them or not.

That means *everyone* is a Dad joker, even if it's by accident.

So it's inevitable that you will make puns, even if you (and everybody else) don't notice them.

**There was a test to join the rowing team, but it just had one "either oar" question.**

***Sigh* I'm all alone. My wife went on a garden tour with some of her best fronds.**

**A double-negative is a definite no-no.**

The *Journal of General Psychology* once published a study that found "a positive relationship between intelligence and joke comprehension." Yet despite all of this wonderful news, there are those who would try to stop us from using our highest brain functions. These meanies include:

1. The Soviet Union, which tried to enforce "one-meaningness" into official communications back in the 1930s. Called

*odnoznachnost*, this approach was designed to destroy ambiguity. Words and statements could mean *one* thing—no more! (George Orwell called this approach "Newspeak" in his dystopian novel, *1984*.)

2.  Modern China, where people regularly get in hot water with officials for using innocent words that might be defined in different, possibly "subversive" ways. To protest these restrictions, citizens use seemingly innocent phrases or names that are actually sophisticated homophonic or visual puns. For example, Winnie the Pooh became a symbol of resistance after memes compared the bear to the Chinese leader Xi Jinping.
3.  Some of my Facebook friends, who have mercilessly discouraged me from making puns.

The forces of repression are everywhere!

## Hey, if a country built lots of dams, it would be a "dam nation."

We have established that you are a borderline genius (got a passport?), but your keen intelligence is a double-edged sword. Corporations are constantly trying to hack your mind with ads specifically designed to take advantage of your mad skills. But while you might appreciate it when a clever advertisement doesn't insult your intelligence, perhaps we're giving these ads too much credit.

For example, M&M's commercials often show two cartoon candies talking to each other. One is the smart candy (the red M&M). And not to sugarcoat it, but the, er, less intelligent candy is the yellow peanut M&M.

Yep, the yellow M&M is a peanut brain. So is that a hidden pun designed to get me to like M&M's more? Or just dumb luck?

It's a mystery wrapped in milk chocolate and covered with a candy coating. And here are some other times when questions arose about the intentionality of punniness:

1. Charmin's toilet paper ads feature bears. Bears don't use toilet paper. But thinking about bears using toilet paper immediately makes one ask the age-old question: "Does a bear poop in the woods?"

   *Verdict*: Joke probably not intended.

2. In *Raiders of the Lost Ark*, Karen Allen's character used a frying pan to knock out a bad guy with a giant knife. So did that mean "the pan is mightier than the sword"?

   *Verdict*: Pun probably not intended.

3. In Frank Herbert's science fiction novel *Dune*, the spice, melange, can triple the human lifespan. And since "mélange" means "a mixture," Herbert could be saying that "variety is the spice of life."

   *Verdict*: Joke possibly intended.

4. In the original *Flash Gordon*, the aliens had guns that shot gloves that could strangle their enemies. So, they were *handguns*.

   *Verdict*: Pun probably intended.

5. In *The Incredibles*, the family's last name is Parr. In golf lingo, par is "average."

   *Verdict*: Pun almost certainly intended.

6. In the film *Clue*, Professor Plum says, "I work for U.N.O., the United Nations Organization, and its special branch, the World Health Organization."

    That stands for UNO WHO.

    *Verdict*: Pun intended.

7. Alan Moore's *Watchmen* pursues the theme of how to make sure that superheroes who enforce the law actually follow the law. That's why a recurring line in the story is the Latin phrase *Quis custodiet ipsos custodes?* ("Who watches the watchmen?") Also, one of the superheroes used to be a watchmaker.

    *Verdict*: Pun intended.


**I've got an idea for a story about a sword fighter with a time machine. It's called "Cut-and-Past."**

**The Saint Nick competition is canceled. Turns out everyone had signed a non-compete Claus.**

**"Bring me my glasses, and step on it!"**
**\*crunch\***

# Know Your Dad Joke

## SPOONERISM

This is what happens if you switch words or parts of words with each other inside a sentence. A famous example is "I'd rather have a bottle in front of me than a frontal lobotomy." A personal example came from when I was artfully organizing cheese and cured meats for an antipasto tray. My wife, Lynn, came in:

**LYNN: It looks like you've finally matched your meat.**
**ME: Did you mean 'met your match'?**
**LYNN: No.**

Spoonerisms (aka, *transpositional puns*) are named for William Archibald Spooner, who often made this error in a public setting. For example, Spooner is said to have baptized twins named Kate and Sydney as "Steak and Kidney." A longer example of this kind of spoonerism is a short Shaggy Dog joke (see next chapter for full explanation):

**A groundskeeper at Buckingham Palace who specialized in growing turf decided to steal the royal throne and hide it in his greenhouse. But he was caught so quickly, it went to show that people working in grass houses shouldn't stow thrones.**

A spoonerism can also simply switch words in a sentence, or switch their usual placement. Like this:

**What's the difference between something you step on to reach high shelves and a 3D printer? The former is a ladder, and the latter is a former.**

A spoonerism can be called a "Russian reversal" if a noun normally does something to another noun, but in the joke, that order gets switched. The comic Yakov Smirnoff pioneered Russian reversals: "In America, you can always find a party. In Russia, the Party always finds *you*."

It's not usually a Dad joke, but I should mention the "unspoken transpositional spoonerism." These usually start, "What's the difference between X and Y?" And they almost always have a bad word as the punchline, yet the punchline is never actually said. Examples:

**"What's the difference between a clever spoonerism and flatulence? One's a shaft of wit, the other a . . . "**

**"What's the difference between a lousy archer and a constipated owl? One can shoot but not hit, the other one . . . "**

# *Shaggy Dogs (and Other Animals)*

### *Q. How does a ferret mail a letter?*
### *A. Very weaselly.*

Hey, did you know that a short, witty comment by a dog would be a *bon mutt*?[1] But its opposite would be a Shaggy Dog. It's a long, seemingly endless tale that concludes with:

1. A punchline, often a pun.

*OR*

2. An anti-joke. (For example, a Shaggy Dog might end with its main character getting unexpectedly run over by a train for no reason.)

Dad jokers usually avoid conflict, but Shaggy Dogs are controversial enough to make us pick sides. Its enthusiasts enjoy drawing out the agony of a long joke and find Shaggy Dogs ideally suited for long car trips with a captive audience.

**"It will be a perfect romantic evening," he thought, lighting a candle. Then he turned and bent down to light another, and accidentally burned his butt on the *first* candle, which caused him**

---

**1.** That's funny because the French term for a witty comment is *bon mot*.

**to spin around and singe his butt on the other one, too. It's rough burning your end on both candles.**

This is clearly inhumane and therefore has its merits:

**True Story: In my entire life, I've jumped and slam dunked on a regulation basketball hoop once. It was a weakish slam with a slightly underinflated ball, but hey, I have witnesses! Sadly, I haven't been able to do it again, so I guess I'm out of bounds.**

Shaggy Dog detractors argue that the beauty of a Dad joke is *timing*. The idea is that you should get in and out quickly— before your audience can erect defenses—but a Shaggy Dog joke can't generate surprised outrage. Instead, they breed a resigned boredom. It's like watching someone jamming together the wrong jigsaw pieces for ten minutes, and then saying "Ta-dah!"

However, I think everyone agrees that the Kid's Unintentional Shaggy Dog can be charming. It's what happens when children tell jokes that accidentally become Shaggy Dogs, with a mangled punchline in the middle of the joke, and extra information still arriving at the end: "No wait, I forgot to tell you that the ostrich was out in the yard! Here, let me start over from the beginning . . ."

LOL, you've gotta love it!

Here's a decent Shaggy Dog joke that's been shortened so as not to annoy:

**A professor of philosophy hired a crew to pour new sidewalk cement in front of her house. Her two children had asked if they could write in the cement, but the professor denied this request.**

Yet while the concrete was drying, the two children ran out and began writing their initials in it anyway.

"What did I say?" the professor cried out. "You two just lost your screen time for the week."

"Oh, that's so harsh, Mom! Don't you love us?"

"Yes, but in the abstract, not in the concrete."

Public Service Announcement: The longest joke in the world has the punch line of "Better Nate than lever." So if someone starts telling you a joke using a character named Nate, look out. Also, beware of Bavarian cream pies and jokes that have to do with "the aristocrats." (Trust me!)

And for the love of Pete, don't tell or listen to Shaggy Dogs that rely on lots of names. As soon as I hear a story like that ("Luke was on his boat, the *Fourth of July*, waiting for his friend Opie . . .") I know it's going to end badly. And let me save you ten minutes by giving you that Shaggy Dog's punchline: "O. B. Juan's kin, Opie, saved Luke from falling to the dock side of the *Fourth*." Ugh.

The University of Connecticut's sports mascot is the Huskies. That's a breed of sled dogs normally found in the Yukon. Get it? University of Connecticut? UConn? Huskies?

## *Know Your Dad Joke*

## FEGHOOTS

A *Feghoot* is a short science fiction Shaggy Dog story. It's named for Ferdinand Feghoot, a character created by Reginald

Bretnor (writing as Grendel Briarton) for a series called "Through Time and Space with Ferdinand Feghoot!" The end of a Feghoot can sometimes be a thing of beauty. For example, one story concludes with three words: "Hungarian ghoul ash." Another pithy one: "non-compass mantis."[2]

Here are a few examples of Feghoot endings; you can probably reverse-engineer a story to fit these pretty easily.

**One man's meat is another man's poi, son.**

**The little fish is his herring aide.**

**Bards of a fetter flog to get 'er.**

**I cannot free the sorest for the tees.**

**You can't make an amulet with out-breaking eggs.**

But enough Shaggy Dogs! Animal rights are my pet passion, so let's talk about them next.

**Did you know that a hive's newborns are called babees?**

**If you went back in time and saw a giant reptile with bad eyesight, what would you call it?**
**A doyouthinkitsaurus.**

**"Aren't you worried woodpeckers will damage your new wood sign?"**
**"Not really—my spelling has always been impeckable."**

---

**2.** These refer to "Hungarian goulash" and "non compos mentis" (Latin for "not of sound mind").

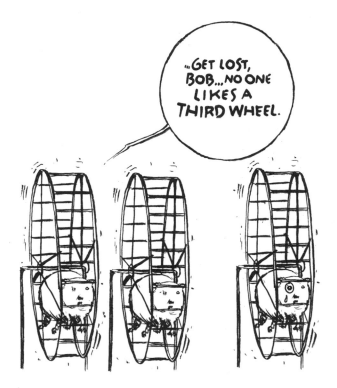

Did you hear about the goats that ran away from home? Don't worry, they're now safely pasture-ized.
*rim shot, explosion*

Of all the crustaceans, I dislike abalone the most. (They're just so incredibly shellfish.)

"Seedy," said the ornithologist, when asked what part of town was best for birdwatching.

I want to open a store that sells only twenty-gallon aquariums. It'll be called "Tanks All the Same."

**"LOL, Nigella failed in front of the whole class while trying to make a brief description of a short-winged diving seabird."**
**"Auk-word!"**

True story: After our new rescue dog left a puddle in the house, I said, "My pup runneth over." Speaking of which, that same dog once ran by my chair and barked his shin. How ironic! And that reminds me, there really is a device that claims to translate your dog's barks for you. It's called Bow-Lingual.

I debated including any bear jokes in this book. Sure, bears are cute, but I didn't want to panda to my audience. And writing about a bi-polar bear's mood swings seems sort of mean. So I'll compromise, and just pull this old Dad joke out of hibernation:

**Why isn't a koala bear a real bear?**
**It doesn't have the right koala-fications.**

**How do nest-building birds get the first few twigs to balance?**
**They use twigonometry.**

**The cuttlefish is one of nature's most misunderstood animals. Sure, it's a tentacled monster, but all it really wants to do is cuttle.**

**I finished a story about a fish who discovers a new memory-enhancing method. It's called *Finding Mnemo*.**

**Some pigeons just brawled in front of me, and now they have a new leader. I think I may have witnessed a "coo d'etat."**

**"I'm going to bring my minnows over to the campfire now."**
**"C'mon, Bill. We have bigger fish to fry."**

The idea that my dog could retrieve a ball that I've thrown as hard as I can is pretty far-fetched.

The seahorse is the only fish with a neck, but I don't want to saddle you with any more useless information.

Never remove a snail's shell. It's mean and it makes them sluggish.

"Look, there's three dog poops in our yard that people didn't pick up!"
"That's quite a phew."

A crow goes shopping in Boston:
"Will this be cash?"
"No, put it on my credit cawed."

In 2019, a UN refugee agency set up an elephant response brigade in Southeast Asia to help deal with problems between humans and wild elephants. It called the new brigade the "Tusk Force."

"Ladies and gentlemen, our Small Horse Auction begins shortly. Please have your funds available and be ready to pony up."

"Hey, that dog ate my wedding ring!"
"So there's a diamond in the Ruff?"

Do not let anyone interrupt when you tell the following joke about flightless birds, or your timing will be thrown off. (In other words, be unflappable.)

The Emu War was a real war that was very inhumane. After all, being mean to the emus made them feel totally ostrich-sized.

# Know Your Dad Joke

## THE WELLERISM

A Wellerism is named after the character Sam Weller, from Charles Dickens's *The Pickwick Papers* (1836). It's usually a line of dialogue with self-referential wordplay. For example:

**"I see," said the blind man, as he picked up his hammer and saw.**

**"We'll have to re-hearse that," said the undertaker as the body tumbled from the coffin.**

**"It comes back to me now," said the girl, spitting into the wind.**

**"Re-markable," said the teacher, trying out her new dry-erase board.**

**"I'm spreading another load of mulch," the gardener re-peated.**

**"I left the newborn kittens behind," the villain said with abandon.**

**"I stand corrected," said the woman in the orthopedic shoes.**

**"How dare you impugn my beard size!" he bristled.**

My favorite variety of Wellerism is the *Tom Swifty*. It's credited to writer Edward Stratemeyer (1862-1930), who wrote and oversaw the production of hundreds of children's stories about the Hardy Boys, Nancy Drew, the Bobbsey Twins, and Tom Swift.

In order to avoid having to keep using the phrase "Tom said" over and over, Stratemeyer liked an adverb-heavy style. Here's one that I like (because I wrote it):

"I hate postal carriers," Tom insisted doggedly.

And here's a lot more!

"This hot dog's good," said Tom frankly.

"You're from the future!" said Tom presciently.

"Let's explore the tomb," Tom said cryptically.

"Pass me the shellfish," said Tom crabbily.

"It's the outside of a tree!" Tom barked.

"I love vegetables," said Tom broccoli.[3]

"Did you walk right up to the victim and shoot him?" Tom asked, point-blank.

"We have to amputate," Tom said disarmingly.

"I might as well be dead," Tom croaked.

"I'm not pregnant," Tom said unexpectantly.

"I just inhaled my fishing lure!" said Tom with bated breath.

"Show no mercy killing the vampire," said Tom painstakingly.

"Hurry up and get to the back of the ship!" Tom said sternly.

"The harbor markers are burning!" Tom yelled flam-buoyantly.

---

**3.** Just checking to see if you're paying attention.

"I TORE UP ALL MY VALENTINE CARDS," SAID TOM HALF-HEARTEDLY.

"I don't know what groceries to purchase," Tom said list-lessly.

"I'm going to go play the organ," Tom piped up.

"I decided to come back to the group," Tom rejoined.

"I didn't do my math homework," said Tom, nonplussed.

"The sun's gone down," Tom said shadily.

"I dropped my toothpaste," Tom said, crest-fallen.

"The exit is right there," Tom pointed out.

"I manufacture table tops," said Tom counterproductively.

"I hear the woodshop teacher had an unfortunate accident," Tom said offhandedly.

Kimberly Baer wrote the best Tom Swifty I've ever seen.[4] Check it:

"Nurse, I need more blankets, and my water pitcher is empty, and also my bedside lamp isn't working," Tom said coldly, dryly, and darkly, yet at the same time patiently.

---

**4.** It was a submission to the Bulwer-Lytton Fiction Contest (p. 169).

# Snarkers Gonna Snark

**1. No puns.**
**2. No puns.**
**3. No puns.**
**—John Cleese's Three Laws of Comedy**

It's sad, but not everyone shares our enthusiasm for wordplay. In the words of Julie Beck, "Punners gonna pun and pun-shunners gonna shun." And those pun-shunners are always going to look at Dad jokes as the verbal equivalent of a tuxedo T-shirt.

But c'mon! Critically acclaimed comedies like *Arrested Development, The Simpsons, BoJack Horseman, Bob's Burgers, Archer,* and *My Little Pony: Friendship Is Magic* are awash in puns and Dad jokes. Yet somehow there are people who claim to "hate puns with a passion." That seems like an odd obsession, doesn't it? Imagine being at a job interview and being asked what you *really* care about.

*You*: My passions include my love for my family, my desire to protect the environment, and the burning hatred that I feel for puns, which permeates every cell of my being.

*Interviewer* (busily taking notes): Your *bean*? LOL, pinto or black?

*You*: This interview is over.

At its worst, a pun is a "benign violation"—a joke that tweaks normality in a harmless way. So why the hate? It's hard to say. As a master of wordplay, Lewis Carroll was aware that some people look down their nose at puns. The sniffy caterpillar in *Alice's Adventures in Wonderland*[1] sums up their attitude:

*Why, Dolly, you have made a pun.*
*But still a pun I do detest.*
*'Tis such a paltry, humbug jest*
*They who've least wit can make them best.*

Carroll's 1876 poem "The Hunting of the Snark" tells the tale of an imaginary creature also possessed of an allergic reaction to a joke:

*Should you happen to venture on one*
*It will sigh like a thing that is deeply distressed:*
*And it always looks grave at a pun.*

Today, the word "snark" means an "unnecessarily snide and sharply critical attitude." And did you see that? It's *unnecessary*. Perhaps snarks sneer at puns because that's the easy, hip, ultra-ironic stance to take. To a guileless Dad joker like you, this probably seems like a weird attitude. There are an infinite number of smiles and laughs available in the universe—so why be stingy about using them?

---

**1.** Fun Fact: *Alice's Adventures in Wonderland* was banned in China in 1931, on the grounds that "animals should not use human language."

**You:** I hate to pry, but can I borrow a crowbar?

**Snark (disgusted):** Only one person in a thousand would laugh at that.

**You:** Looks like you missed your chance to be special!

**Because I felt low today, my friend said, "Cheer up, it could be worse. You could be stuck underground in a hole full of water." I know he means well.**

A second explanation for haters is that while a pun is harmless, it *does* require puzzling out. That entails a bit of work before the final "A-ha!" payoff. So I suppose that having to work for a joke might cause resentment. Along those lines, we've established that it takes courage and creativity to make a Dad joke. But criticizing one? That's easy. You have nothing on the line, and it's always easier to tear something down than build it up.[2]

I HATE TO **PRY,** BUT MAY I **BORROW** YOUR **CROWBAR?**

---

**2.** You know what they say: A critic is someone who pans for gold.

**"Hey, how did you get into the prestigious Puppeteer Academy?"
"Oh, I just pulled a few strings."**

A third possibility is that some people—even the funny ones—think of themselves as too classy for this nonsense. They prefer their wit dignified and unpunned.

In her novel *Mansfield Park*, Jane Austen only wrote one pun, and it's there to show that the Dad joker in question lacks character. P. G. Wodehouse was extraordinarily funny, and he didn't use puns. And when Mark Twain's story "The Celebrated Jumping Frog of Calaveras County" came out, reviewers jumped favorably all over it because the tale was funny without being punny.

**HUMAN CANNONBALL: I quit!
CIRCUS LEADER: But where will I find another person of your caliber?**

My final theory is that maybe some people just don't get it. Seriously, they don't get the joke. Then when they *do* get it, they don't like that they didn't get it. Either these people hate surprises, or they think it's an insult to their critical thinking skills. For example, I remember speaking with an acquaintance at a birthday party when this happened:

**ACQUAINTANCE: The woman over there started her own law firm last year, but it's too soon to tell whether it'll succeed.
ME: So the jury's still out?
ACQUAINTANCE: ...
ME: ...
[beat]**

**ACQUAINTANCE (frowning): Har-dee-har-har.[3]**

Snarky!

Of course, none of my theories explain why a genius like John Cleese isn't a pun fan. He's a good reminder that there are wonderful people out there who just aren't down with Dad jokes. But John Cleese *does* think that the best puns involve other languages. So in the interest of cultural exchange:

## Know Your Dad Joke

## *MACARONIC PUNS*

Someone once told me the Italian word for suppository is "innuendo," and it took me ten minutes to get it. Italian offers many other opportunities for cross-language puns; like, if you want to make eating at your work station glamorous, call it "*dining al desco.*"

A joke using a word from another language is often called a *macaronic* pun. How charming and cosmopolitan![4] Macaronic comes from the Italian word *maccarone*, which my research shows is both a pasta and a slang term used for . . . simpletons and dolts.

Like I said: Charming. Cosmopolitan.

---

**3.** Oof. The only thing worse than a "Har-dee-har-har" is a "That's so funny, I forgot to laugh."

**4.** Along those lines, Yiddish has been called the "tongue that never takes its tongue out of its cheek."

Anyway, if you eat a gross sausage and say "This *wurst* is the worst!", you've made a macaronic pun. Now see if you spot the pattern in these macaronic examples:

**The French poodle ate a *haute* dog.**

**You know why they only eat one egg for breakfast in France? Because in France, one egg is an *oeuf*.**

**Paris is a site for *soirees*.**

**I am so relaxed about rules, you could say have I have a certain *blasé-faire*.[5]**

**The father of your archenemy is a *foe pa*.**

**In the US, the National Security Agency's parties have a certain "*je NSA quoi*."**

Did you spot the pattern? LOL, I was just kidding. There isn't one. But English has more than a million words, and so many of these words come from other languages, you *could* argue that any pun is macaronic. And charming. And cosmopolitan. (Okay, I'll stop.)

One of the most influential Dad joke haters was Karl Marx, who called puns a sign of the "lumpen proletariat." Since jokes about communism aren't funny unless everyone gets them, here are some question/answer puns that even a Bolshevik would love.

**How many Marxists does it take to screw in a light bulb? None—the light bulb contains the seeds of its own revolution.**

---

**5.** This is funny because *laissez-faire* means to let things take their own course, without interfering.

What kind of fish did Marx hate?
Czardines.

Why did the Russian regiment have a hard time hitting targets?
They had poor Marx-manship.

A communist and a fascist are sitting on the porch of a nudist colony.
The communist asks, "Have you read Marx?"
The fascist says, "Yeah, I think it's these wicker chairs."

So who's the lumpen proletariat *now*? Fine, it's me. (BTW, do you know why Karl Marx always wrote in lowercase?)[6]

When it comes to tough audiences, it's hard to imagine a tougher one than the Prussian military leader Helmuth von Moltke. He was reported to have only laughed twice—and one of those times was after being told his mother-in-law died.

Yet the philosopher Martin Heidegger reportedly only laughed *once*. It happened when Heidegger and Ernst Jünger went for a picnic. When Jünger leaned over to pick up a dropped sausage roll, his lederhosen seat split open. Heidegger guffawed, then reverted to being a professional philosopher for the rest of his life.

Bummer.

Even the famous *New Yorker* editor William Shawn qualified as a snark, at least on the job. Shawn once cut a passage where a writer was interviewing a man about how he got around the city. The man said:

**"Diesel."**
**I said, "Diesel?"**
**He pointed to his feet and said, "Diesel get me anywhere."**

Shawn explained to the writer why he deleted that bit: "I think you must not understand that to use this pun would *destroy this magazine*."

Please. Using a pun won't destroy *anything*.

---

**6.** Because he hated capitalism.

Probably![7]

You know how there's nothing more rewarding than being super-polite to rude people? It's even better to troll snarks with puns. Who knows, it might loosen them up. And even if it doesn't, at least you'll get some enjoyment out of it.

## DISSIN'-FRANCHISE

Thinking about pun haters got me thinking about Hollywood. (Just work with me on this, okay?) See, sometimes Dad jokes are hiding in plain sight, and many of these invisible jokes come from the world of entertainment. For example, the first episode of a TV show is a *pilot*, as it's the first to air. Get it? Get it? But we're so used to what was once a joke, it's just sort of invisible now.

Anyway, with regard to wordplay, there are three kinds of TV shows and movies.

1. Some avoid Dad jokes like the plague. It's like Jane Austen was in charge of them or something.
2. Some slyly embed their puns. I remember watching a rerun of *Star Trek* where Captain Kirk meets a librarian named Mr. Atoz. "I get it!" I thought. The joke is right there: A to Z.
3. Some trot out Dad jokes without compunction. The vintage James Bond films were full of awful puns, like the scene in

---

**7.** Except the English language, according to Samuel Johnson: "To trifle with the vocabulary . . . is to tamper with the currency of human intelligence." Johnson also said that "Puns are the last refuge of the witless," which is totally untrue. (They're our *first* refuge.)

*Live and Let Die*, when a villain literally blows up and Bond says, "He always did have an inflated opinion of himself."

To conclude this section, let me say that I am a fan of *Guardians of the Galaxy*. In fact, if you give me a pencil, I can sketch a great Groot. (Drawing stick figures is easy.) And when I meet real-life snarks, I compare them to the fictional character, Drax, who takes everything literally.

*Rocket:* Metaphors are gonna go over his head.
*Drax:* Nothing goes over my head! My reflexes are too fast, and I would catch it.

Thinking of Dad joke haters as being like Drax helps me to understand and forgive them. More importantly, it helps me enjoy them. And hopefully you can enjoy this handful of pop culture Dad jokes. (Or should that just be "Pop culture"? Get it? Get it?)

**We had a special party to celebrate the new Star Wars movie. It was a canon ball.**

**FRODO: I've decided to leave the Shire.**
**SAM: But Master Frodo, why?**
**FRODO: Gentrification has made it un-in-hobbit-able.**
**[both laugh and hoist tankards of mead]**

**"Hey, it's a message from Thor! But I can't read it."**
**"Why not?"**
**"It's in Norse code."**
**"Way to rune the moment."**

Q. How many ears does Mr. Spock have?
A. Three. The left ear, the right ear, and the final frontier.
—Cash Ashkinos

"You once were a ve-gone, and now you will *be* gone."
—Scott Pilgrim, after defeating his vegan adversary in *Scott Pilgrim vs. the World*

"Up, Up, and Oy Vey!" —Superboy, after his bar mitzvah

If a new character is unsuccessfully introduced in a fast superhero's comic book, is he a pan in the Flash?

I was disappointed to learn that ent-omologists don't study sentient, walking trees.

In the original manuscript of *The Lord of the Rings*, J. R. R. Tolkien had a wandering minstrel with swiveling hips named Elvish Presley.

I always thought the name "Frodo" had a nice ring to it.

"Holmes, how did you know I had indigestion?"
"It's alimentary, my dear Watson."

Oh, and I almost forgot to say: There are a few dedicated Dad jokers who like numerical order puns. For example, consider the theatergoer who asked for a movie ticket like this: "One to see Saw Five in six at seven."[8]

---

**8.** Or "One to 3-D Thor in five at six."

# Know Your Dad Joke

## PORTMANTEAU

A portmanteau is a word that creatively combines two or more other words for a new meaning. Ex. "The rich woman was easy to talk to, and she immediately seemed like a famillionaire."

Some portmanteaus are so common, we forget they were once special, like biopic ("biographical picture"), smog ("smoke" and "fog"), cosplay ("costume play"), and Spam (actually, nobody knows *what's* in Spam). Some of my favorite portmanteaus include adorkable, bizarrchitecture, and turducken.

A *malamanteau* is a portmanteau done wrong. It was invented by Randall Munroe, of "xkcd" fame. Example: "She showed impressive cussplay at the comic convention."

# Science and Medicine

> **"As you know, organic chemistry is the study of organs, like the Wurlitzer [and] the Hammond Electric. . . . Inorganic chemistry is the study of the insides of organs."**
> **—Max Shulman**

People who know science know humor. As evidence, I submit this statement from a scientist at the Centers for Disease Control and Prevention:

**"I'm seeing an uptick in Lyme disease cases."**

Interestingly, a team of computer scientists from Stanford University created a pun generator and is working on building Artificial Intelligence that would be naturally funny. And (no joke) the team is led by a scientist named He He.

But employing and artificially creating humor isn't enough for scientists. They need to *understand* it. That's why two scientists did a computational model of humor comprehension. (This is not the set-up to a joke.) To do this, they decided to use homophonic puns in the data set that participants would respond to. These puns included:

**Italian building inspectors in Pisa are leanient.**

**A criminal's best asset is his lie ability.**

**Be kind to your dentist because he has fillings too.**

**Atheism is a non-prophet organization.**

As you can see, the meaning of the "pun" word makes sense in the context of those sentences. And given that setting, test subjects could easily identify jokes and non-jokes. So the key to a good pun? Context! While that sounds pretty obvious, always be sure to ask yourself if *your* audience can do the same. And if you are concerned that they lack the necessary context to get your joke, do one of the following:

1.  Prior to making your joke, say, "Before you hear this really great joke, you need to know that . . . " (This is a great way to prime the comedic pump.)

OR

2.  As you already know, you can follow up your joke by saying, "That's funny because..."

OR

3.  Just laugh at your joke and ignore your audience's uncomprehending look of resentment.

As the following science-oriented Dad jokes lack context, they will also be missing a certain charm. Read them anyway!

**There's no way around it—the Flat Earth Society exists. But give credit to its members for being brave: the only thing they have to fear is sphere itself.**

Black holes are fascinating. It's a subject that really draws you in.

Nurses have excellent academic credentials.
They're members of the IV league.

I thought there was a full moon tonight. If not, it'll happen lunar or later.

"Why are there neurons and dendrites hung on frames everywhere?"
"It's been a nerve-racking day."

A number of physicians who own unrented apartment buildings are forming their own group. It's called Doctors Without Boarders.

I entered an astronomy competition and won the constellation prize.

Did you hear about $1/2$'s denominator visiting its numerator? It wanted to see how the other half lived. Then there was the teen who got trapped inside $3/4$. (It was a minor in-fraction.)

DOCTOR: You're repeatedly getting nasty infections in the same spot.
PATIENT: So I'm . . . ?"
DOCTOR: Abcess-ive compulsive.

Hey, did you hear that someday soon they're going to change the definition of a kilogram?
. . . Weight for it . . .

The Dermatologists Club:
"You're treating a butterfly expert with bad acne?"
"Yes, but it's hopeless. A lepidopterologist can't change his spots."

"Did you go to the nursery?"
"No."
"Well, it's hard to plant a garden if you haven't botany."

"So you're saying my salivary glands are over-producing?" I gushed.

"The woman who invented Kevlar died. Vest in peace." —Ed Yong

In physics, the persistence of apathy is called "the conservation of 'don't matter.'"

From *The Simpsons:*
PRISON WARDEN: I mean, look at this! It's a unicorn in outer space! I mean, what's it breathin'?
HOMER: Air?
PRISON WARDEN: Ain't no air in space!
HOMER (grins): There's an Air 'n' Space Museum. (He gets thrown out of prison.)

In some circles, it's common to know the value of pi.

Would you like to join the Cloud Appreciation Society? Yes, I'm cirrus.

The rule "I before E except after C" has been disproved by science.

Did I ever tell you about when I did a charity walk for equal rights and tore my ACLU?

Vivisecting yourself is a real "I" opener.[1]

"Ow, I broke my thumbnail!"
"But on the other hand, you're fine."

Kids, don't stick a fork in that outlet, or you're grounded.

"Midwives help people out!"
—Bumper sticker I saw

After running a diagnostic on the chemist's scales, I showed her the error of her weighs.

In hindsight, I should have bought more toilet paper.

"Over here is a silo of healthy corn. And next to it is a bushel of rotten barley."
"I get it. You're playing good crop, bad crop."

Spoiler Alert: Items in your compost bin are decomposing.

I wanted to post a joke about salt, but I was like, Na, people won't understand.

"I refuse to write about geology, because it's beneath me. And meteorology is over my head."
"Why not be a little boulder, and give it a try?"
"Gneiss pun. I salute you, of quartz."

---

**1.** This is funny because vivisection is the act of dissecting something that's still alive.

PRO TIP: At your next surgery, ask "Does anyone need anything while I'm out?" right after they give you anesthesia.

DERMATOLOGIST: How was my chicken pox diagnosis?
PATIENT: Spot on.
DERMATOLOGIST: Funny. Do you know why I don't like surgeons?
PATIENT: No.
DERMATOLOGIST: Too many inside jokes.
PATIENT: I meant, no, don't tell me. Now I might be breaking out again.
DERMATOLOGIST: If you don't like my jokes, that's okay. I have thick skin.
PATIENT: Normally, I have a lot of respect for someone like you who's built up their own business from scratch.
DERMATOLOGIST: Why are you leaving? Don't do anything rash—
[door shuts]

My sister-in-law told me that some pregnant women look for suitable tide pools to give birth in. So once a good pool is found, is it designated a "sea-section"?
*large wave washes me out to sea, people cheer*

Did you hear what the talking dog said to the doctor?
"Physician, heel thyself."

I'm angry to learn that my medical biopsies had been stolen, then infused into aromatic, flammable sticks. In fact, I am incensed!

True Story: In the course of visiting someone at the VA hospital, I helped a gentleman get to the restroom. Afterward, his wife said I had answered "the call of doody."

After my dentist told me to do a better job, I was at a floss for words. Then I felt a chill as she adjusted her mask and said, "It's time for a cavity search."[2]

**Chemistry Class:**
STUDENT 1: Uranium, Argon, Nitrogen, Arsenic.
STUDENT 2: Huh?
STUDENT 1: U, Ar, N, As.

## Know Your Dad Joke

### URANUS

This planet is an obvious choice for cracking jokes. Depending on how you feel about poop humor, making this planet the butt of your jokes may be irresistible. (Also, Jon Stewart says Lake Titicaca is the Uranus of lakes, so enjoy.)

"Junior, please keep your fingers out of your nose."
"Sheesh, Mom—picky, picky, picky!"

---

**2.** This is funny because a dentist would search for cavities, but a "cavity search" is something that law enforcement officers do to make sure contraband isn't being smuggled.

BONFIRE OF THE MANATEES...
Miami Herald
FLORIDA CONSERVATION FAILURES

# Headlines

**"Scooby Doom: Puppy blows up owners' house after chewing through can of deodorant"**
**—Headline in Metro (UK)**

If you're looking for the most current Dad jokes, who better to sum up a news story with a punchy joke than a journalist? Reporters are *so* good at puns, their headlines sometimes get nixed for having too much awesome. For instance, take the article about Florida's conservation failures that was initially titled "The Bonfire of the Manatees."[1]

Knowing how this can happen, I sometimes like to make up my own headlines for articles. Like how an article about a killer flu should have been called "Phlegm Fatale."

Or that time when *Billboard* ran an article on the Hu, a Mongolian metal band, it read "The Hu Brings Mongolian Metal

---

**1.** This is funny because Tom Wolfe wrote a novel called *The Bonfire of the Vanities*. Along these lines, Evelyn Waugh wrote a novel satirizing England's secret societies in 1928. Almost 90 years later, news broke that as an Oxford student, British Prime Minister David Cameron engaged in a secret society ritual involving a pig's head. This led Hari Kunzru to write an editorial titled "Waugh Pigs." (That headline got spiked, as nobody at the *New York Times* is a Black Sabbath fan.)

to No. 1 on Sales Chart." But anyone can see that should've been called "Hu's on First"![2]

Along those lines, when a story broke that scientists had detected earthquakes on Mars, Marina Koren called it "The Fault in Our Mars."[3]

Song titles and lyrics provide excellent sources of material for headings. For example, any piece about goat rental agencies should be titled "We Got the Bleat." Other real-life samplings:

**"How Do You Solve a Problem Like Korea"**

**"Scrape Me Up Before You Go Slow" (a story about George Michael getting into a freeway crash)**

And then this, from an article about a *really* expensive railroad construction project:

**"Is this the real price?**
**Is this just fantasy?**
**Caught up in land buys**
**No escape from bureaucracy"**

Music also inspired what's considered history's greatest Dad joke headline. In 2000, the Scottish semi-pro soccer team, Inverness Caledonian Thistle, defeated the mighty Celtic squad. This major upset led to this headline in the *Sun*:

**"Super Caley Go Ballistic, Celtic Are Atrocious"**

---

**2.** This is funny because "Who's on first?" is the name of a famous comedy bit by Abbott and Costello.

**3.** And yes, I know they're actually *mars*quakes.

Wow. Just wow. Sticking with sports for a moment, a baseball journalist caught a headline-drive in 1963. After watching an easy pop-up land for a base hit because of bad communication between Philadelphia Phillies infielders Bobby Wine and Cookie Rojas, the reporter came up with "The Daze of Wine and Rojas."[4]

Here are three of my very favorite headlines.

1.  When politician Michael Foot was named to lead a group working toward nuclear disarmament, the story ran as "Foot Heads Arms Body."
2.  I can't remember if I dreamed this, but I'm pretty sure that once I saw an article about depressed cats that was head-lined "Woetry in Meowtion."
3.  And when Chris Rock filed for divorce, Holly J. Morris wrote this ro-sham-bo-dacious headline: "Rock's papers scissor union."

More works of genius follow; British tabloids and the *New York Post* have the lion's share of them:

**"Underwear Bandit Caught, Admits Brief Crime Spree"**

**"Otter Devastation"** (An article about otters eating local chickens and fish.)

**"Glass Eye Is No Help Identifying Corpse"**

**"Rubble Without a Cause"** (The cause was actually an earthquake, but I still like it.)

**"Man Who Snatched Wig Will Have Toupee"**

---

**4.** But I bet he was tempted by "That's the way the Cookie Crumbles."

"Shouting Match Ends Teacher's Hearing" (This may have been an accidental pun.)

"Will and Kate Release Fresh Prints of Swell Heir"

"The Liar, the Witch and the Wardrobe" (A man faked his own death, then continued living in a studio that he accessed through his wife's wardrobe.)

"Store-bought Hair Dye Can Make Hair Die"

"From Russia . . . With Gloves" (A winter storm from Russia hits Europe)

"Can Incontinence Be Treated? Depends"

"Pair Charged with Battery"

"Two Convicts Evade Noose; Jury Hung"

Finally, I just read a story headlined "Flock of sheep helps police end ninety-minute car chase in New Zealand." (It raises the question: why didn't the offender just make a ewe turn?) And my hat's off to this headline for a story about tightrope walkers who ventured across the Han River in Korea: "Skywalkers in Korea Cross Han Solo".

# Great Moments in Dad Joke History

## THE TIME CAPSULE

A gentleman named Ryan Kramer posted the following note with a photo online:

"Five months ago, my roommate John moved out. I haven't been in his room since then, however this week, behind a tiny door that accesses a water valve, we found a little surprise. [It was a fake mustache.] After sending John a confused text, he replied by saying, 'You found it! My secret 'stache!'

"He had been waiting five months to make that pun."

# Punning Through the Ages

## *"In the beginning was the pun."*
## *—Samuel Beckett*

When I was a kid, if one of my classmates told an old joke, we'd say, "The last time I heard that, I fell off my dinosaur."

Man, we thought that was funny.

Just how old are Dad jokes? Visual puns have been dated to 35,000 years ago, and legitimate Dad jokes have likely existed as long as written language. Anyone with an interest in the matter should turn to John Pollack's fascinating book, *The Pun Also Rises.*[1] In it, Pollack details the evolution of language and wordplay through history, including how punning may have led to the invention of alphabets, which he calls a "pun-intended consequence."

There was no shortage of ancient Dad jokers. Plato enjoyed puns. Unfortunately, he shouldered so many philosophical tasks, he was unable to indulge his tastes. (That is, he just had too much on his Plato.)

---

**1.** "The son-in-law also rises." —MGM studio employee, after Louis B. Mayer appointed his daughter's husband to an executive position.

Aristotle wrote about puns in *Rhetoric*, saying that "the joke is good if it fits the facts." And Mediocrities was an ancient Greek philosopher who came up some of the earliest and least impressive Dad jokes.[2]

For the record, here are two of history's earliest examples of wordplay:

1. From ancient Sumeria comes the epic saga of Gilgamesh. In it, the gods get angry with humans and decide to flood the earth. However, one mortal was tipped off about the upcoming deluge, and he was told to do two things:

    a. Build an ark (sound familiar?)[3], and . . .
    b. Tell his nosy neighbors that it was going to rain *"kibtu"* and *"kukku."*

    Here's the catch. *Kibtu* and *kukku* were words for corn but also puns on the Mesopotamian words for sorrow and bad luck. So maybe there's a kernel of truth to Dad jokes being corny.

2. The ancient Greeks told tales of the Oracle of Delphi, a seer known for giving cryptic advice. Because the seer's words were double-edged, it was wise to give them careful analysis. Consider the Greek general who went to the Oracle for input and was told *"Domine stes"* (stay at home).

    In Greek, that sounded like *"Domi ne stes"* (don't stay home), so the general went to war and was promptly killed.
    Oops! Teehee.

---

**2.** His talent was so marginal, he didn't actually exist.

**3.** BTW, Noah kept his bees in the ark-hives.

(The Greeks also told of Charon, who ferries dead souls across a river to the underworld of Hades. It was a boring job, but does Charon give up? No, he Styx with it.)

The Greek poet Homer's love of puns shows in *The Odyssey*. (And no, his writing is not "Homer-oidal.") In this tale, Odysseus and his companions get trapped in the cave of a man-eating Cyclops named Polyphemus.

When asked for his name by the monster, Odysseus answers, "I am No One."

Odysseus and his crew then manage to put out Polyphemus's eye and escape the cave while disguised as sheep. (Don't ask.) Later, when the Cyclops's brothers ask who blinded him, Polyphemus yells, "No One! No One has blinded me." So the other brothers tell Polyphemus to quiet down if no one is to blame, and Odysseus escapes.[4] (As a wag has noted, Polyphemus should have written his tormentor a note: "Eye hate ewe, No One.")

**True Story: I met a girl named Cassandra who refused to "Apollo-gize" for her horrendous Greek myth puns. But no worries—I still took her seer-iously.[5]**

For many ancient peoples, wordplay wasn't really "play" at all. Think of the life-or-death outcome for those who were riddled by the Sphinx in the myths. And in real life, being able to prove

---

**4.** When he eventually returns home, Odysseus actually has to pretend he *is* nobody to avoid being assassinated. Irony!

**5.** This is funny because in Greek mythology, Cassandra was a seer who could tell the future, but was cursed to have nobody believe her prophecies.

intellectual superiority could be as good as winning a fight. In the Western Hemisphere, the Mayans were big fans of puns, employing them in verbal duels involving riddles and rhymes, sort of like a modern day rap battle. And out in the Pacific Ocean, the Hawaiians also had contests with complex riddles and wordplay, sometimes in the form of oral duels that had fatal consequences for the losers.

**It's likely that Egyptian hieroglyphics show visual puns. (Speaking of which, ancient Egyptians always knew when their ruler was approaching. They could smell his Pharaoh-mones.)[6]**

Perhaps the first book of puns was written by Roman politician Cicero (106 BCE–43 BCE). It definitely did not contain the following dialogue:

**VISIGOTH: Long day?**
**ROMAN CENTURION (at desk): Oh, I'm just working IX to V. How are you feeling?**
**VISIGOTH: I just learned how to write 51, 6, and 500 in Roman numerals, so I am LIVID.**
**CENTURION: LOL. Are you planning on any pillaging today? No? Guess I don't have to call IXII.**
**VISIGOTH: Let me know if you need help cutting up those papyrus sheets. I have a great pair of Caesars.**

Maybe the most famous pun in history came when Jesus said that he would build his church on top of Peter. He didn't mean it literally, because that would be cruel, and he was . . . y'know,

---

**6.** I sphinx this is a good one.

Jesus. But once I learned that the Greek translation of Peter is "rock," well, ISWYDT.[7]

## Medieval Prison:
## "What're you in for?"
## "Chain-mail fraud."

In the Middle Ages, feudalism was the dominant social structure. Its motto: "It's your count that votes!" And of course, heraldry became popular back then. The idea was that a coat of arms would symbolically reference a family's name and history. This was known as "canting arms," and that's why today's members of the Society for Creative Anachronisms say, "Heralds don't pun. They cant."

In modern times, Sir George Martin was the producer of many Beatles albums, and his coat of arms has beetles on it. And Princess Beatrice of York's crest shows three bees. "Bee-a-trice"—get it? (If the princess were an apiarist, she'd be a real keeper.)

You could argue that flags are just heraldry for nations; some have elaborate colors and designs, while others are the model of simplicity. For example, Switzerland's flag is all red, with a white cross in the middle, so that's a big plus.

It was back in the fourteenth century that the Black Death hit. Since all the cool kids were getting the dread disease, some children just pretended to have it as well, but that was total plague-iarism.

---

**7.** Jesus famously said, "Come forth and I will give you eternal glory." Unfortunately, Peter came fifth, and so just won a turtleneck sweater.

## Medieval Parenting: "Go to your loom!"

As London became a major world city in the 1500s, puns in the English language grew in popularity. The most notable of the era's wordplayers, William Shakespeare, averaged 78 puns per play. (*Romeo and Juliet* has 175 puns, while *Love's Labour Lost* has 200.) These high ratios of witty wordplay helped maintain the audience's interest.

## The Taj Mahal is nice, but you can't afford it. The price would be monumental.

Some of Shakespeare's puns are silly, lots are sexual, and some are grim. Take Hamlet's bitter joke about his uncle: "A little more than kin, and less than kind."[8] (And if you've never heard of *Hamlet* before, that's a tragedy.) I'm also partial to the part in *Romeo and Juliet* where the dying Mercutio says, "Ask for me tomorrow, and you shall find me a grave man."

## Sure, Joan of Arc got the burning headlines. But her cousin, Timothy of Sphere, was a well-rounded person.

The modern person who claims to appreciate all of Shakespeare's jokes is either a PhD in Elizabethan literature or is full of Bardloney. Many Shakespearean references depend on archaic terms, or persons and events that have misted over with time. Even so, it's estimated that perhaps half of Shakespeare's puns are still understandable to us today. And that bit in *Julius Caesar* about a cobbler being a mender of bad soles? That still totally works.

---

**8.** It's funny because his uncle killed Hamlet's father, then married Hamlet's mother, thus becoming Hamlet's stepfather. (Wait . . . that's not funny at all.)

**As you know, in 1492, Columbus sailed the ocean blue. What you may not know is that he got almost 2,000 miles a galleon.**

In 1528, an Italian named Baldassar Castiglione wrote a book describing the perfect gentleman titled *The Book of the Courtier*. It praised witty charm and devoted a section to puns. Castiglione also warned against telling jokes that "fall flat and seem too labored."

No Dad joker, he.

Puns lost cachet during the Scientific Revolution, when there was a movement toward being exact in one's terms. The muddying effect of a pun was considered poor taste in some circles, and so a rhetorical device that had once been highly thought of started to become something to apologize for.

But pun fans struck back with a satirical pamphlet called *God's Revenge Against Punning: Shewing the Miserable Fates of Persons Addicted to This Crying Sin*. It humorously put puns on the same level as disasters like the Great Fire of London and the Black Death.

As for the word "pun," it may be a seventeenth century slang descendant of the Italian word *puntiglio* (a fine point). However, there's also good evidence that "pun" is actually a shortening of the Sanskrit word "pundit," which originally meant a "wise, educated Hindu." If so, the word was transported from India by English sailors who also stowed away other vocabulary words like *shampoo, guru, jungle,* and *wit*.

In 1785, Thomas Sheridan wrote a poem in which Zeus creates humans as *living puns*: androgynous creatures with a "two-fold" nature. No, not origami, but male and female:

*"So much alike, so near the same,*
*They stuck as closely as their name.*
*Whatever words the male expressed,*
*The female turned into a jest;*
*Whatever words the female spoke,*
*The male converted to a joke:*
*So in this form of man and wife,*
*They led a merry punning life."*

Oh, and the Victorians were well known for their puns. Typical example: "Why should the number 288 never be mentioned in company? Because it is two gross."

## *YANKEE, GO PUN*

Dad jokes were so popular in North America, they almost prevented the United States from getting properly founded.

The year was 1787, and Thomas Jefferson had *had* it. There were so many puns being launched at the Constitutional Convention in Philadelphia, Jefferson was starting to lose his belief in democracy. The nation's leaders were *supposed* to be figuring out their system of government, but instead, they just kept making jokes. In a letter to Abigail Adams, Jefferson complained:

*"The most remarkable effect of this convention as yet is the number of puns . . . it has generated. I think were they all collected it would make a more voluminous work than the Encyclopedia. This occasion . . . convinces me that this nation is incapable of any serious effort but under the word of command.*

*The people at large view every object only as it may furnish puns . . . and I pronounce that a good punster would disarm the whole nation were they ever so seriously disposed to revolt."*

But for every Thomas Jefferson killjoy, there was a jolly Benjamin Franklin cracking wise. (His "We must all hang together or assuredly we shall all hang separately" is so familiar, it's easy to forget that it's a Dad joke.) Other notable Dad jokers included Davy Crockett, Henry David Thoreau, and Alexander Graham Bell. But the mack daddy of them all was:

# Dad Joke Hall of Fame:

## ABRAHAM LINCOLN

Abraham Lincoln loved tall tales, jokes, and puns. After seeing a woman wearing a plumed hat slip and fall in a puddle, Lincoln (before offering assistance) is said to have remarked, "Reminds me of a duck. Feathers on her head, down on her behind."

On suspending the death sentence of a man: "If I don't suspend it tonight, the man will surely be suspended tomorrow."

And after being jokingly asked to contribute to a fund to buy an attorney new pants after he split his pants seat: "I can contribute nothing to the end in view."

Abraham Lincoln made no secret of the fact that he didn't attend college. This came in handy when Lincoln debated Stephen Douglas in Galesburg, Illinois, in 1858. It was a frigid, windy day, and the debate site was Knox College. To shield the candidates from gusts, the stage was between two campus buildings, and to get to it, the debaters had to climb through a first-floor window.

After doing so, Lincoln said, "Well, at last I have gone through college."

## *THE GREATEST DIS IN PUN HISTORY*

While there are ample political puns, they are often pretty dreary. Calvin Coolidge ran for president with the slogan "Keep Cool and Keep Coolidge." Okay. During the 1932 campaign, Franklin D. Roosevelt's supporters made badges in the shape of his famous dog Fala that urged voters to "Fala me to the polls." Fine. And later, Eisenhower's voters proudly proclaimed "I like Ike." I mean, I guess that's a pun?

HOWEVER . . .

While Dad jokes are friendly, and put-downs are not our thing, an exception must be made for the politician Horace Mann. An abolitionist, Mann was criticized in 1850 by Senator Lewis Cass for not being in favor of letting states decide whether slavery should be allowed in their territories. And in his attack, Senator Cass made a pun on Mann's name.

This was a fatal mistake!

Horace Mann responded: "Did it not occur to the [Senator Cass] that his own name offers the most grievous temptation for punning?" And then Mann let loose with the following:

*This Ass is very big. Then call him CAss;*
*C's Roman for 100;—a hundred times an ass.*

That's funny because the Roman number for 100 is C. Therefore, in this insult, Senator Cass's *own name* makes him "a hundred times an ass." Or, to put it another way:

## YEAH!!

Horace Mann suggested that if Senator Cass would lay off the puns, he would "draw no more upon the asinine or Cassinine associations which his name suggests." And thus ended the matter before further blood was spilled.

In the first half of the twentieth century, vaudeville and Borscht Belt entertainers relied heavily on Dad joke material. While puns came to be widely used in advertising, even as late as World War I, wordplay was still somewhat new to the marketing game. The Ford Motor Company even put on a contest with cash prizes for advertising slogans, but warned, "We do not care for puns."[9]

As for World War I, it was horrible, but seasoned veterans who had survived pepper spray and mustard gas used dark humor to cope. For example, they sometimes described trench warfare as a "last-ditch effort." And soldiers did the same thing in World War II. A Dad joke making the rounds then: "What kind of breakfast does Hitler eat?" "Luftwaffles." (When Germany took over Czechoslovakia in 1939, a short man went to the British embassy and requested asylum by saying, "Would you mind caching a small Czech?")

One last World War II reference: My friend Chris once noticed that a companion seemed to be shielding his nose when

---

**9.** And in a weird coincidence, Henry Ford was a total jerk.

speaking. He explained that he'd shaved poorly, and there was some facial hair just under his nose.

"Does it look bad?" he asked.

"Nope," responded Chris. "Just a little Führer o'clock shadow."[10]

Over the course of the twentieth century, the carefully constructed punny joke slowly came to be considered less funny and more corny. Yet today, Dad jokers still seem to exist in one form or another worldwide. In Korea, the word *ajae* is used for the middle-aged folk who make unfunny jokes (often puns) to youngsters. Japan's version of this is the *oyaji gyagu,* a person who gets more enjoyment from telling jokes than their audience does from hearing them.

And who knows? Perhaps on a planet orbiting some distant star, a group of small pseudopods are yelling, "Da-ad!" at a larger tentacled creature who's saying, "Get it? Get it?" (Then the little pseudopods push the big one into a spaceship and send him into orbit.)

**World's Worst Tourism Slogans:**
**"Djibeauty" (for Djibouti)**
**"GREAT Britain"**
**"I feel sLOVEnia"**

**"An appreciative murmur ran through the audience, but was hurriedly grabbed by an attendant and shown the door." —Peter Cook**

---

**10.** "This joke falls outside of *Mein Kampf*-ort zone." —Myq Kaplan

I'm petrified of becoming an old fossil.

ME (seeing a vintage sports car): Look, it's a Triumph.
MY WIFE (unimpressed): I'd say it's a qualified win at best.

# Food and Business

*"Time flies like an arrow; fruit flies like a banana."*
*—Old joke*

'Sup?

I'm working on a snack-related project, so can you hang on for just one second? Okay, after crunching the numbers, I know I've eaten eleven corn chips.

Thank you.

Now to set the mood, I'm going to cue up some "R & Brie."

Of all possible topics, food puns might be the easiest to make and the most satisfying. There just seems to be an endless series of quips out there to be harvested. For example, this zinger that my wife zinged:

**ME (at the produce stand): Do you want pink ladies, cameos, or gala apples?**
**LYNN: Get the cameos. They only make a brief appearance.**

If I may, I'd like to take a moment to salute the food cart owners and restaurant proprietors who have followed their dreams. One of my favorite food carts was Comfortably Yum. Kudos also to the proprietors of the Greek diner named Aesop's Tables, the

Vietnamese restaurant named 9021Pho, the falafel shop called Pita Pan, and the fish-and-chip shop called Frying Nemo.

Oh, and I just got an idea for a United Nations lunch café called the Delegate-essen. I also wouldn't mind opening a Wiccan sandwich shop called 'Wich Craft. And if I ever open a barbecue rib joint, it'll be called Sears. But when it comes to invented names for eating establishments, I've got nothing on writer Dale Basye. He wrote a short story about the United Noshes Food Carts, which includes such gems as:

**Lotso Matzo**

**Falafelly Good**

**Wurst Case Scenario**

**Papa's Got a Brand New Baguette**

**Dressed to Kielbasa**

**Viet Nom-Nom**

**Nicolas Cajun**

**Thai Food Mary's**

**In Spain in the Membrane**

**Crepe Chute**

**The Gyro of Living Dangerously**

**Curry-ocity Killed the Cat**

**Bench Shawarmas**

**The Unbearable Lightness of Beans**

Oh, I meant to ask: Have you ever seen a Wienermobile? For more than thirty years, six of these giant hot-dog cars have been touring the country. Each car has two Oscar Mayer drivers on board, one to drive and the other riding "shot bun." Prospective Wienermobile drivers have to prove they can cut the mustard, but once they're hired, they are known as hotdoggers. They always wear a "meat belt," keep the "bunroof" down in nice weather, and they claim to really relish the experience. And if the Wienermobile broke down and a tow truck operator asked the drivers what the problem was, I really hope they'd just point to the car and say, "It needs all the fixin's."

Also, since I love cheese, I was hoping you'd seen video of the famous Cooper's Hill Cheese-Rolling and Wake event in England. To begin it, a large wheel of Double Gloucester cheese is sent rolling down a steep hill. Contestants then chase after the cheese, and they almost always wipe out spectacularly. One year, after a particularly nasty cataclysm, all that was left at the end was de brie.

**Weird Al Yankovic once co-wrote a cheese-and-movie themed crossword puzzle for the New York Times. It included answers like "A FEW GOUDA MEN," "FETA ATTRACTION," "QUESOBLANCA," "FONDUE THE RIGHT THING," and "CHEESY RIDER."**

Not to brag, but I'm sort of a natural in any kitchen. Since I instinctively know where everything is, I guess I'm just counter-intuitive. Yet my wife has even better skills than I do. She just baked a delicious-smelling cake, then said that I can't have a piece yet. (But if I have to wait much longer, there's going to be a mutiny on the bundt-y.)[1]

---

**1.** This is funny because a Bundt® is a type of cake, and *Mutiny on the Bounty* is a famous book that's been made into a number of films. (Also, my wife really did just bake a cake, so there.)

Anyway, I cherry-picked some of my favorite Dad food jokes below. *Bon appétit.*

Important: If anyone ever says "hominy grits," you are obligated to say, "Hundreds!"

I tried to make my own smoothie, with mixed results.

"I hate it when you put dried fruit in the cookies."
"You're being unraisin-able. Most people like fruit."
"Then I guess I'm going against the currant."

Hang on, I have to give a shout-out to this soup: Booyah base!

At the concession stand:
Customer: This popcorn's stale and its butter is rancid.
Clerk: I concede your point.

After dropping the sliced cabbage salad at a picnic:
"You've heard of Murphy's Law? This was Cole's Law."

"I don't want to hear another Peep out of you!"
—Parent scolding child who got sick overeating Easter candy.

Someone spit out an apricot stone, and I slipped on it. (Gotta hate those pitfalls.)

"He who spelt it, dealt it."
—Motto at a gluten-free bakery.

After the mayor endorsed her bread, the baker realized she was the toast of the town.

Salad at a friend's house:

"Okay, I washed everything, so I think all of this produce is safe to eat."

"You *think*? Then lettuce will romaine off-limits."

"But surely you won't leaf the spinach all alone?"

"Sorry, but it'd be a kale-amity if your food were cress-contaminated."

If you're at a sushi restaurant and you're going to order squid or octopus, be sure to say, "Let's get kraken!"

At the food warehouse:

"Boss, I can't use the forklift on those candied yams."

"Why not?"

"They're unpalletable."

I was really hungry for a baked pastry, plus I ran out of my seaweed supplements. But luckily, a nice neighbor lent me what I needed. (I get pie with a little kelp from my friends.)

The problem with getting dysentery in equatorial regions is that things start going south quickly.[2]

I want my wife to explain how to make her homemade dough. But she tells me I'm on a "knead to know" basis.

"Don't try to butter me up—I'm a vegan."
—*Broad City*

---

**2.** That's funny because . . . actually, you're gonna have to look that one up.

Sorry for dropping the cherry tomatoes and then cursing. It was just a slip of the tongs.

If disliking ham jokes is a sickness, I don't want to be cured.

I searched the kitchen for a banana or apple, but my quest was fruitless.

I just bought some "collector's edition" ice cream. It's in mint condition.

"What are these bananas doing in the fridge?"
"They're cooling their peels."

Thirsty? Espresso is worth a shot.

Just saw a guy in the coffee shop wearing a cap-and-chinos.

Not to be fuzzy on the details, but would anyone like a fresh peach?

"Hey, I told you not to borrow my kitchen tools!"
"It was a whisk I was willing to take."

Somebody make me an alligator sandwich. And make it snappy!

There's a movie coming out about a vampire who snacks between meals. It's called *Nosh-feratu*.[3]

Why yes, an article on Iraqi bakeries headlined "Fertile Croissant" would be terrific.

---

**3.** This is funny because "noshing" is snacking, and *Nosferatu* is a famous vampire film.

"Remember when I stood on that bakery's gigantic bun?"
"Yeah, you were really on a roll."

"Would you like some escargot?"
"No thanks. I prefer fast food."

Me: The microwave just broke.
Father-in-law: So we're going cold turkey today?

Me (standing in a line, holding a cup): Dang, all these people beat me to the punch.

Amanda sliced the top and bottom off the salami and pushed them together so that she could make ends meat.

"Does this steak meet FDA standards for chewability?"
"Yes, it's legal tender."

"Have you been eating all my fresh fruit?"
"Oh, stop being so pear-anoid."

While I don't usually drink tea, I'm not a total tea-totaller. But the problem with imported tea is that the prices are just too steep.

## GETTING DOWN TO BUSINESS

Hang on, all this food talk made me remember another great restaurant name: *Thaitanic*! But if I had to start a business, I'd go with a furniture shop called Sofa, So Good. (Motto: "We have the one nightstand you'll never regret.") Either that, or I would specialize in footstools with a place called Ottoman Empire. And although I am bald, I could be talked into financing a hair salon that would be called either Hairosmith or Curl Up and Dye.[4]

**On a trip to Ireland, novelist Paul Auster spotted a law firm named Argue & Phibbs.**

There apparently is a mall in Moldova called Malldova, which brings me to my Dad Joke Business Name awards. In absolutely

---

**4.** But a mattress-and-mutton shop called Bedlam(b) is probably too specialized.

last place is the "botox beauty bar" known as Ject. When you go there, you are "in Ject." Get it? (Don't get it.) Not to nitpick, but third place goes to the business that specializes in delousing children known as Lice Knowing You.

In second place is the restaurant called Aunt Chiladas.

And my Dad Joke Business Name Award goes to the automotive repair shop called Wreck-Amended. (That name is no accident.)

While the constraints of reality keep most owners conservative with their business names, on the animated sitcom *Bob's Burgers*, the imaginary business next door to the diner changes regularly. Some of these shop names have included:

**You Can't Handle the Ruth, Baseball Cards**

**Granny Packs, Luggage for Seniors**

**Baby Got Back Problems, Physical Therapy**

**Tandemonium, All Your Tandem Bike Needs**

**Happily Ever Actor, Casting Agency**

**Footloose, Prosthetic Adjustments**

**That's A-Door-A-Bell Doorbells**

**Don't Stop Bereaving, Grief Counseling**

**The Nightlight Zone**

**Cat-Like Refluxes, Feline Gastroenterologist**

**I Think Therefore I Jam, Profound Preserves**

**Get Off My Back, Tramp Stamp Removals**

# Upping Your Game

### *"I live and die by puns."*
### *— Feist*

Picture this scenario: You're driving the kids to soccer practice, and you approach an intersection. Braking lightly, you ask,

**"Hey, what does a yellow light mean?"**
**"Slow down."**
**"Okay. Whaaaaat dooooooes aaaaa yellllllow liiiiight meeeeeean?"**

This is a Hall of Fame Dad Joke, but it has a "tell by" expiration date. At the age of three, a kid might not get it. For the same kid at five or six, this joke kills. Yet over the ensuing years, there will be diminishing returns on the joke until it gets to the point where they don't respond to it at all.

**Anytime you put the car in reverse, you should say, "Ahh, this takes me back."**

**If you should see cows, quickly say, "Look kids, a flock of cows."**
**One of them will correct you: "A *herd* of cows."**
**Then you say, "Of course I *heard* of cows, there's a flock of them right there."**

That makes sense: it's part of every kid's job to eventually cringe at their parents' humor. The important question is, what do *you* do? Do you just keep making the joke, doubling down on it, trying to recapture the magic of a bygone time when you were a demigod? Tragically, many Dad jokers get trapped in that futile, sweet nostalgia.

But there's another possibility: why not let your Dad jokes grow as your child grows? That way, your humor doesn't get left behind like a bygone plaything from *Toy Story*. If you choose to change with the times, your jokes will have to change, too. Simply put, they'll have to be a bit more sophisticated.

Consider how every book starts as a mystery. You start reading not knowing exactly where the book is going to lead, and you create a narrative based on the context the author provides. Your jokes are the same way. You start presenting information to your audience, and then they have to put together the puzzle and recognize that there is a joke there.

## Know Your Dad Joke

### PARADIGMATIC HUMOR

Any joke where the audience has to know outside context to "get" the joke. For example:

1. An inside joke.
2. Humor that requires knowledge of history, pop culture, science, or some other field to understand.

**Ex. In monosyllabic societies, you have to take a lot for grunted.**

I'm pretty sure that almost all jokes that don't involve making faces or weird sounds are paradigmatic jokes, but some are more paradigmatic than others. For example, when a polar vortex hit the Midwest in 2019, local performances of the musical *Hamilton* were canceled. That led Andrew Conneen to observe, "Brrrr kills Hamilton again."

That's brilliant if you know that Aaron Burr killed Alexander Hamilton in a duel. Otherwise? Meaningless!

## Dad Joke Shout-Out

### SPONGEBOB SQUAREPANTS

In one episode of this fine program, Squidward tricks Patrick and Spongebob into carrying him everywhere. But everywhere they go, Squidward complains that things are "too wet" or "too wet" or "too whatever." When the group stops in front of an underwater version of a Moulin Rouge poster, Squidward says, "Too-loose Lautrec!"[1]

---

**1.** It's funny because the painting closely resembled the style of the famous French painter, Henri de Toulouse-Lautrec.

## BUT WHAT IF THEY DON'T GET IT?

Norton Juster's children's book *The Phantom Tollbooth* is packed with wordplay.[2] There's a bird in it called the Everpresent Wordsnatcher, and it's from a place named Context. The Everpresent Wordsnatcher likes to take people's words and twist them around. As it says: *"I'm from a land very far away called Context. But it's such a nasty place I try to spend all my time out of it."*

For you, the tricky thing about coming up with new material for your Dad jokes is that your kids may not get the context. So they'll think you're just being weird when you are, in fact, trying to torture them to build character. How can you ensure that they have the knowledge necessary to follow your joke's path of association?

If you think of a great joke but know that your audience won't get it, take the time to explain the joke's context *before* telling the joke. Wait an hour or even a day (but not too long, or they'll forget), and *then* spring the joke.

Of course, this kind of long-range planning requires almost diabolical cunning. Which is why you're the exact right person for the job! And as you seek to redefine your approach, consider redefinitions themselves as a source of humor.

---

**2.** In *The Phantom Tollbooth*, there is a carriage that "goes without saying." So as soon as all its passengers are quiet, it starts moving.

# Know Your Dad Joke

## NEW MEANINGS

The *Washington Post* has hosted a variety of wordplay contests, such as when readers were asked to slightly change a word's spelling to give it a new definition. Results included:

**Giraffiti (n):** Vandalism spray-painted very, very high.

**Sarchasm (n):** The gulf between an ironic joke and the person who doesn't get it.

**Neo-fight (n.)** What happens when two pacifists lose their cool and clumsily go after each other.[3]

Another contest asked for Dad-joke versions of actual words:

**Egomaniac:** Someone who's always me-deep in conversation.

**Igloo:** An icicle built for two.

**Jacket blurb:** Fable of contents

**Sunbather:** A fry in the ointment

And of course, you can use the *sound* of the word to make the joke:

**After the woman bumped into me, I told her to loquacious going.**

**I know a tailor who will make Machiavelli good suit for a decent price.**

---

**3.** Okay, that one's actually mine. Don't like it? Fight me.

One can also find new uses for words by following an already established pattern. For example, lawyers get *disbarred* for misdoing. Ministers are *defrocked*. So perhaps teachers are *degraded*, mediums are *dispirited*, electricians are *delighted*, accountants are *disfigured*, and cowboys are *deranged*.

## *HIGH-BROW DAD JOKES*

I watched incredulously as the man finished clipping his cuticles at Aunt Joan's open-casket funeral.
"That's the last nail in the coffin," I thought.

AUCTIONEER: Do I hear any bids?
ME: *Adieu.*

I've decided my new year's resolutions work better in tiff than in jpeg.

"Mom, Dad, I believe the universe can only be understood when I rest my body on the joints between my thighs and lower legs."
[both parents gasp]
"But Billy, that means you're—"
"A kneel-ist."

"Marx spots the ex."
—Groucho Marx, on seeing his former wife in a restaurant.

Taking an afternoon nap facedown is something I'm prone to do.

Going to a lousy party is a *fête* worse than death.

"Why are you surrounded by smiling armed escorts?"

"Because I want to be guardedly optimistic."

When Tyrone got the strangely heavy piece of furniture home and opened it, three people fell out. It was apparently a missing persons bureau.

"These walls were not built to scale," said the prison's architect.

"What's your degree in?"
". . ."
"Are you going to answer?"
"You're asking a Rhetoric question."

If the best part of your email comes after your sign-off, you have a real *P.S. de résistance*.

"There is a sad gentleman from Bavaria staying with us."
"Oh, a Germanic depressive?"

"[He's] been awarded the electric chair of philosophy."
—Christopher Hitchens, on the murder conviction of a philosopher.

"Hey boss, do you want my stamp collection?"
"Philately will get you nowhere."
"Ah, you saw through my plan. But I am happy to cajole and fawn; I will even kiss up a wheedle bit."[4]

Steve Brooks is the inventor of a philosophy known as "Tex-Mex-istentialism."

---

**4.** This is funny because stamp collecting is called *philately*, which sounds like "flattery." And *wheedle* is a verb for charming someone, and it also sounds like "little."

College Linguistics Department:
"Professor, I understand that after years of research, you can now speak with mice."
"Oh, I just squeak by."

"It is what it is," said the faux-losopher.

You know who had a killer digital strategy? The Boston Strangler.[5]

Being coerced to join an undeserved standing ovation is a real clap-trap.

Two years ago, I rode my bike over double yellow lines, wiped out, and was temporarily parallelized.

At the Law Firm:
"Thomas, I didn't like that con you pulled at the reading of the will."
"What'd I do?"
"You were putting on heirs."

If a little kid dresses as a spy for Halloween, are they an agent prova-cute-ur?

Spun honey is the most inhumane product ever. Do you have any idea of what a centrifuge does to a beehive?

My dad is studying ancient Greek, so for his eighty-first birthday, I had a cake decorated with "χαρούμενα γενέθλια" (happy birthday).

---

**5.** Just checking: did that one give you pause? It should have, because it's not a Dad joke! Remember, your material should be family friendly and relatively harmless. (I still like the joke, though.)

But despite my thoughtfulness, Dad denied me a slice, saying, "You can't have archaic and eat it, too."

After her parents bought a Möbius strip-shaped house, Serena always felt out of the loop.

She glared accusingly from beneath her mortarboard. "I don't appreciate you giving me the third degree."
"But you majored in business, economics, and aerospace engineering," said the university dean. "Most people would be happy to receive three diplomas."[6]

After purchasing the oval Chinese cooking skillet from the diminutive British aristocrat, Nigel realized he had taken a long wok off a short Peer.

# *LITERATURE*

My wife and I used to attend the Oregon Shakespeare Festival, and we once stayed in town at an Airbnb run by a woman named Beth. Since I'd forgotten my dental floss, I called out, "Oh, Beth, where is thy string?"[7]

That reminds me that I've made it this far into the book and I haven't shared my favorite Shakespeare Dad joke. It's from *Hamlet*, Act II, Scene ii.

*Polonius:* What do you read, my lord?
*Hamlet:* Words, words, words.

---

**6.** This joke is so creative, it *starts* with the punchline.

**7.** This was my greatest moment as a human being.

Over the course of time, so many distinguished poets and writers have loved wordplay, it's hard to know where to start. Dorothy Parker and Nancy Mitford were experts at it, and Sophocles, Rabelais, Montaigne, and Wittgenstein were all pun enthusiasts. So were the following luminaries:

• John Milton wrote *Paradise Lost*, and in it, Satan puns twelve times in nine lines. (And it's hella funny!)

• John Keats said on his deathbed, "I summoned up more puns, in a sort of desperation, in one week than in any year of my life."

• Samuel Taylor Coleridge: "All [those] who possess . . . imagination and a philosophical spirit, are prone to punning."

• Jonathan Swift wrote *Gulliver's Travels*, a book that is actually populated by Houyhnhnms (homonyms). Swift also wrote a piece called "Regarding The End," which deals with both death *and* butts. Not only did he write his own defense of punning, but Swift perhaps lent a hand to the writing of the 1719 booklet, *The Art of Punning*.

• Oscar Wilde's reputation as an untamed punster is unimpeachable. Ex. "Immanuel doesn't pun, he Kant."

• Jean Paul Sartre praised the pun's "intellectual freedom." And another existentialist, Samuel Beckett, relied heavily on wordplay; the name of his most famous work, *Waiting for Godot*, is arguably a pun.

• Sigmund Freud called the pun a "victorious assertion of the ego's invulnerability." (He also called the Christmas season the "alcoholidays.")

• James Joyce loved using macaronic puns, which makes reading his novel *Finnegans Wake* even more ~~awful~~ rewarding.

• G. K. Chesterton called the pun an "ancient and often barbaric kind of humour." (He liked them.)

## LITERARY DAD JOKES

Here's a reading pun pattern that you can pattern your patter after:

**I just read a book about nerve damage. It left me with bad feelings.**

**I just read a book about a bank vault. It was hard to get into.**

**I just read a book on anti-gravity. It was impossible to put down.**

I'M TRYING TO KNEEL...

BUT I THINK I'M BUZZED...

ANTI-GRAVITY FOR DUMMIES

**I just read a book about an infallible baseball player who worked on a mound. It was pitch perfect.**

Come up with your own line for this book! (And to make this extra challenging, don't use any expletives.)

Regarding authorship, Sarah Woolsey was an American children's writer who wrote under the pen name "Susan Coolidge." So I guess that was her Sue-donym.

As for me, I considered having my authorship for this book be Thorin Gremlinoski so that I could have a gnome de plume.

And I just realized it would've been cool if Samuel Clemens could have talked to Shakespeare, but I guess never the Twain shall meet.

By the way, I am an excellent guest. When I visit someone's home and there are books around, it speaks volumes. (Even though someone was bound to make that joke, it still makes my spine tingle.)

**One of the most intuitive characters in fiction was Quasimodo. He had a magnificent hunch.**

**"Hello, you've reached Cheever Books."**
**"Is your bookstore multistory?"**
**"Nope."**
**"But you can't do very well if you only sell one story."**
**\*hangs up\***

That novel you wrote in second person is still waiting for a second person to read it.

"I loved *Wuthering Heights*. On a scale of one to ten, it was at least a nine."
"Wow, that's a really good wuther report."[8]

Good news! If you are a fan of writer Umberto Eco, you're Eco-friendly.

It's really annoying that the people who write all these post-apocalyptic books apparently don't understand the meaning of "apocalyptic." Armageddon mad!

Why yes, you could call a book pirate a "tome raider."

The inmate in the prison's writing class considered the prose and the cons.

*The Art of Fielding* by Chad Harbach is a novel about playing baseball and growing up. It's what the Germans call a *Bildungs-homerun*.

"Do you like Kipling?"
"I don't know. I've never kipled."

Herman Melville once called the US a "seat of snivelization."

In 1934, a book came out titled *How to Run a Bassoon Factory*. It was a must-reed.

---

**8.** Did you know that Charlotte Brontë was just 4 feet 9 inches tall? Small wonder she didn't write *Wuthering Heights*.

"No, dummy, I need a people doctor."
—The last words of Max Baer, on being told the hotel's house doctor was coming.

"What's up with Tolstoy?"
"It's a long story."

POETRY PROF: Break up this line with one stressed and two unstressed syllables.
STUDENT: I should 'tear-a-dactyl'?
PROF: You're expelled.

If you wrote poetry about immoral behavior, it'd be vice versa.

True Story: James Joyce boycotted vowels for some of the dialogue in his novel *Finnegans Wake*, e.g:

—Nnn ttt wrd?

—Dmn ttt thg.

Joyce called this "disemvowelled" writing.

The writer Dorothy Parker was capable of cutting puns. After Clare Boothe Luce wrote a self-serving book about World War II, Dorothy Parker titled her review of it "All Clare on the Western Front."

And I really should share that Kurt Vonnegut's novel, *Cat's Cradle*, has a ritual described as a meeting of souls. It is performed by having the two participants removing their shoes, and then pressing the soles of their feet together.

*WARNING*: The cutting edge jokes in this chapter may encourage you to start using dark or risqué humor to seem cool. You may even be tempted to tell someone how back in the eighteenth century, Samuel Johnson and his sidekick, James Boswell, chanced upon a mob of people. What was going on? A member of the crowd told the gentlemen that a convict named Mr. Vowel was to be hanged.

Samuel Johnson turned to his companion and said, "Well, it is very clear, Bozzy, that it is neither U nor I."

This is a fine story, but it's *not* a Dad joke! Actually, you know what? Maybe it is! Anyway, remember, your material should be family friendly and harmless. In order to keep your humor stable and remind you of our core values, please enjoy:

# Dad Joke Shout-Out

## MY LITTLE PONY

I have an idea for a *Dora the Explorer* episode in which she goes into orbit around the Earth. This story would be called "Revolving Dora." Thank you. But there are already so many great cartoon puns that go unacknowledged, I wonder if anyone would even notice my genius? For example, the animated film *Chicken Run* used "Escape or Die Frying" in its marketing campaign—and it still didn't win an Oscar. What an outrage! So let me take a moment to praise the episode titles of *My Little Pony: Friendship Is Magic.* They are pure quality:

"Viva Las Pegasus"

"Bridle Gossip"

"Boast Busters"

"Sonic Rainboom"

"Stare Master"

"The Mysterious Mare Do Well"

"Just for Sidekicks"

"Amending Fences"

"The Mane Attraction"

"No Second Prances"

"Stranger than Fan Fiction"

"Parental Glideance"

# Pun-Pong

*"Puns are little 'plays on words' that a certain breed of person loves to spring on you and then look at you in a certain self-satisfied way to indicate that he thinks that you must think that he is by far the cleverest person on Earth now that Benjamin Franklin is dead, when in fact what you are thinking is that if this person ever ends up in a lifeboat, the other passengers will hurl him overboard by the end of the first day even if they have plenty of food and water."*
**—Dave Barry, Dave Barry's Greatest Hits**

In Shakespeare's plays, puns are often trotted out in competitive circumstances. And as you know, if you make a pun in the presence of another Dad joker, they are legally required to add a pun to yours. Should you then respond in kind, next thing you know, you're playing pun-pong, which is the nerd version of a rap battle. Here's an example that was inspired by an old joke:

**DOCTOR: You're pregnant.**

**YOU: You've got to be kid-in-me.**

**DOCTOR: Please don't abbreviate your words or you'll go into contractions.**

**YOU: Ha. The only way my water is going to break is if I drop an ice cube.**

**DOCTOR: Did you get pregnant just to have this conversation?**

YOU: A-parently so.

DOCTOR: Inconceivable. But seriously, you are going to put on some pounds in the coming months.

YOU: It'll be worth the weight.

DOCTOR: I'm . . . afraid I'm going to have to recommend you to another physician.

YOU: That sutures me just fine.

DOCTOR: Nurse? Call security.

YOU: I guess I have to go now, but it was totally birth it.

If you like playing with others, this kind of conversation is fun. Or it *can* be fun, provided you can think on your feet. As Douglas Adams may have said, "A wit thinks of something funny immediately; a comedy writer thinks of something *very* funny two hours later." And after all, quick punning didn't give the characters in Winnie the Pooh any trouble:

*Rabbit:* Can you tie a knot?

*Piglet:* I cannot.

*Rabbit:* Ah, so you can knot?

*Piglet:* No, I cannot knot.

*[later]*

*Eeyore:* . . . it's all for naught.

But for some people, a punning conversation is like their own private wordplay fight club, and it's ham-to-ham combat. If that's you, ease up already. Nobody likes a competitive Dad joker. In fact, that's the worst possible combination of character traits, right up there with talkative scrapbooker, collector of used tissues, and Pokémon taxonomy expert.

However, if another Dad joker wants to wordplay with you, go along with it with the understanding that you will eventually run into one of two problems:

1. You're trapped in a seemingly never-ending cycle of increasingly bad Dad jokes.
2. You're out of ideas.

Some Dad jokers love to get the last word in, so depending on you, the pun-pong match might go on until the local townspeople break out the pitchforks and torches. My suggestion is that you play along, get in a few good lines, and then beat a hasty retreat. And if that means the other party gets in the last pun, so be it.

But my guess is that the other party will be just as relieved. For instance, let's say you're at work and your colleague sees a protractor on your desk.

**COLLEAGUE: Perfect! I've been looking for a new angle on a problem.**
**YOU: I hate to draw the line, but if you go solve it now, we won't have to protract this conversation.**
**[exit COLLEAGUE]**

That was perfect! You both offloaded jokes, and the conversation didn't turn into a chore. I mean, let's face it: it's tiresome talking with someone who's trying to beat you to the pun when they should just be listening to how awesome you are.

Conversations like these are amateur versions of official punning competitions such as New York's Punderdome or the O. Henry Pun-Off World Championships in Austin, Texas. In these events, contestants are typically given a topic to riff on (e.g.

pet stores). They then try to come up with quality puns on that theme to impress the judges and audience—and to eliminate their sometimes cleverly-named competitors.

Joe Berkowitz wrote about his experiences on the pun competition circuit in the book, *Away With Words*, and some of the contestants' *nom de puns* that he met included:

**Attila the Pun**

**Groan Up**

**Black Punther**

**Do Pun to Others**

**Punda Express**

**Words Nightmare**

**Punder Enlightening**

**The Pundance Kid**

So how can you up your game? Whether you are trying to improve your spontaneous humor skills, hoping to best a pesky neighbor, or entering an official competition, here are some techniques for developing your Dad joke skillz:

- Do crossword puzzles, especially from the *New York Times.* Playing other word games, such as Scrabble and Boggle can't hurt.
- Be childlike! Or immature—your choice. By doing this, you retain a literal and non-literal way of thinking about words and phrases that will stand you in good stead.
- Drink coffee. The caffeine will heighten your sentences.

- Practice improvising material in your head. Do this by giving yourself themes to work on while you pretend to be matched up with an opponent. For example, I just came back from a walk where I was thinking about a pun contest about royalty:

**I guess the two of us are going to duke it out. We'll be baron knuckles and trying to knock the other one down for the count. In the end, only one can be crowned victor.**

Okay, I'll admit that looks pretty lame on paper right now, but that just means that you can do better!

## OCCUPATIONAL HAZARD

There is a type of brain lesion in the right frontal lobe that causes people to take intense amusement from their own compulsive puns. The name for this pathological com-pun-ction is *witzelsucht*, which is German for "wit sickness." (Really.)

In 1846, Oliver Wendell Holmes wrote a story about brain-addled patients titled "A Visit to the Asylum for Aged and Decayed Punsters." (Sample joke: "If he spells leather *lether*, and feather *fether*, isn't there danger that he'll give us a bad spell of weather?")

Now that you've been thinking about Dad jokes, you might contract a tiny, contact-high version of *witzelsucht*. But my guess is that you don't want people to think you need brain surgery by having conversations like this:

"Hi."
"Hi. Hello. Greetings! Good to see you. How's it going? LOL."

"Um . . . what are you doing?"

"Sorry, I got a 'contact hi.' Get it?"

Please don't become the awful kind of person who tries to start a pundemic by inserting endless and often irrelevant jokes into chats and parties. Everyone will hate you if you do this, so take a shot of pun-acillin, enact some pun control legislation, and RESTRAIN YOURSELF.[1]

Remember, your Dad jokes should usually be confined to a select audience. If you always think of "the world" as your audience and then never shut up, people will get used to ignoring *everything* you say, rendering you increasingly irrelevant. It's horrible. In fact, this is how people become invisible in their own families.

Not that I would know anything about that—hey, Mom, wait for me!

## QUALITY PRE-LOADED HUMOR

Dad jokers are enthusiastic recyclers. After all, our kind has been recycling some of the same jokes for thousands of years. Unless you can be a spontaneous genius 24/7, being ready with a quality pre-used quip at a moment's notice is okay. You can reduce, reuse, and repun while you develop your own material. Admittedly, knee-jerk jokes aren't the highest expression of our art form, but here are a few scenarios to get you started anyway.

---

**1.** Otherwise, your friends can sue you for pun-itive damages, and you may be pun-ished by serving time in a pun-itentiary. (Okay, I'll stop.)

If you ever hear someone cry out "Eureka!" retort, "Yeah, well, you don't smell very good yourself."[2]

If you're at your parents' house and one of their guests tells them, "Thank you for having me," immediately cry out, "They're not *your* parents. Sheesh!"

Feel free to carry around a copy of Charles Dickens's *Great Expectations* until someone asks you what you think of it. Then you can say, "It's not what I hoped for."

If someone passes gas:
"I've caught wind of something disturbing."

If you trip in a hole, point to it and say,
"I'm upset by this hole thing."

Anytime someone says, "Watch your language!"
"Uh, English. What's yours?"

Anytime someone asks, "What's that [book or movie] about?
"Oh, it's about [x number of pages or x minutes long]."

If anybody asks. "What's new?"
"The thirteenth letter of the Greek alphabet."[3]

When someone inquires, "What's the big idea?"
"Einstein's unified theory of the universe."

---

**2.** This is a Marx brothers line. (Also, in the *Unbreakable Kimmy Schmidt*, it's always funny when Kimmy cries out, "Urethra!")

**3.** It's Nu.

There are times when you'll be forced to initiate the conversation so that you can feed yourself a line. This is very TTH, so don't overdo it. For example, if the kids are bingeing on a program, you could go with:

**"Did you kids just watch three episodes of that show back to back?**
**"Yes."**
**"Well then who was facing the television?"**
" . . . "

Finally, if anyone ever mentions the name Pavlov, they will *expect* you to say, "That name rings a bell." So try this instead:

**"Do you know why Pavlov's hair was so soft? Because he conditioned it."**

# *Great Moments in Dad Joke History*

## *THE POP STARS*

The beauty of Dad jokes is that there is always a new generation to assume the mantle of leadership. Two inspirational examples are the high school students Kaden Anderson and Quinn Horak. While working in their algebra textbook, the two friends came across this pun:

**The soda bottle took music lessons in order to become a band liter.**

Get it? Band liter? Concerned that an opportunity for a better punchline had been missed, Kaden and Quinn contacted the publisher and gently suggested that future editions use this instead:

**The soda bottle took music lessons in order to become a pop star.[4]**

An editor wrote back a thank-you note and graciously assured the two students that the publisher was "soda-determined" to get the entry right. So kudos to you, Kaden and Quinn! It's Fanta-stic stories like these that give us hope for the next generation.

---

**4.** True, by one metric, this change was missing a unit of measurement, but that IS a better punchline!

# Next Steps: Expanding Your Audience

### *"Pun: A form of wit, to which wise men stoop and fools aspire." —Ambrose Bierce*

By now, you're ready to expand your Dad joke range to the public at large. After all, why should your family and friends be the only ones to benefit from your wit? But before you imagine a successful life in stand-up comedy, I don't recommend that you go to an open mic with your Dad joke material.

There are a couple of reasons for this: legal culpability and the Geneva Convention. A comedy act that revolves around puns just won't work. Trust me.[1] Jo Firestone calls the pun "the annoying younger brother or sister of the comedy world," which is a weird fate for a Dad joke, but there it is.

Luckily, social media can provide a partial outlet for your creativity. If your experience is anything like mine, your puns will

---

**1.** Dad jokes typically don't go over well with a room full of strangers with drinks who are thinking of you as their "night out."

help narrow your bloated friends and followers lists, enabling you to speak to the true intellectuals. (Hi, Dad!)

Also, Reddit has two subreddits (Punny and Dad Jokes) where you can share G-rated comedic gems online. As a tip, Redditors generally like memes and pictures, but short clever posts can also get crowd support. The downside of Reddit is that anonymous strangers might downvote your work. Strike that: anonymous strangers *will* downvote your work. But your loved ones have been downvoting you for years, so I'm guessing an unflattering reaction from someone named Random2129 isn't a problem.

When you're ready for the major leagues, try the fantastic Bulwer-Lytton Fiction Contest (BLFC). But be prepared, because it's a fantastic *bad* writing contest. In other words, the BLFC features the most artfully wretched writing you can imagine. This contest is open to any writer who composes the worst possible opening sentence for what would be a truly awful novel.

For example, an Australian writer named John Wallace went with:

**"Once upon a time, there was a place where things happened; allow me to be more specific."**

Not bad!

Which is to say, pretty bad.

The BLFC crowd-sources awfulness in genres that include children's literature, crime, science fiction, romance, and puns. Here's a sampling of some of its wonders:

"Lois was essentially a tragic case, with her penchant for duck-hunting gamekeepers who inevitably departed with a feather in their cap, whilst she was left feeling down and picking up the bill."
—Anita Bowden

"Locals know it as Pinocchio Rock, because it's shaped like a proboscis, and lies at the edge of the cliff." —John Holmes

"As James King, detective in the Queens branch of the NYPD, stared at the rooks pecking at the disheveled corpse of Bishop Robert Knight in the alley behind the pawn shop, he checked for his mates." —Mark McGivern

"Pet detective Drake Leghorn ducked reporters at the entrance to the small hobby farm and headed down to the tiny pond where a lone goose was frantically calling for her mate and he wondered why—when so many come to look upon the graceful mating pair—why would someone want to take a gander?" —Howie McLennon

"Six months old, and already their love had picked up memories like lint, which, now that Maddie thought about it, was appropriate, since she and Brian met at the laundromat, when Maddie found herself hampered by a stubborn washing machine, but then snickered at the thought of being 'hampered' while doing laundry, and then found herself explaining her snicker to the nearest laundromat patron, who turned out to be Brian and who, better yet, turned out to have a sense of humor even, well, dryer than her own." —Kirsten Wilson

"Using her flint knife to gut the two amphibians, Kreega the Neanderthal woman created the first pair of open-toad sandals."
—Greg Homer

"Detective Kodiak plucked a single hair from the bearskin rug and at once understood the grisly nature of the crime: it had been a ferocious act, a real honey, the sort of thing that could polarize a community, so he padded quietly out the back to avoid a cub reporter waiting in the den." —Joe Wyatt

"Niles deeply regretted bringing his own equipment to the company's annual croquet tournament because those were his fingerprints found on the 'blunt instrument' that had caused the fatal depression in his boss's skull and now here he stood in court accused of murder, yes, murder in the first degree with mallets aforethought." —Linda Boatright

"This is a story of twin Siamese kittens, or, more specifically, of their shared appendage; it is a tail of two kitties." —David Bubenik

"The droppings of the migrating Canada geese just missed the outdoor revelers at the inaugural Asian math puzzle competition, marking the first time that dung flew over Sudoku Fest."
—Kevin P. Craver

"Sven, who rode his unicycle while training for the biathlon, thought the triceratops was the most regal of dinosaurs, exercised in the quad of his apartment complex down the street from the Pentagon, sang in a sextet (he is a baritone), had a deviated septum, fought for fun in the octagon, seemed to have nine lives and spent a decade living with the aborigines, was the kind of man you could count on." —Jeff Green

Created by Professor Scott Rice and sponsored by San Jose State University's English department, the BLFC is named for Edward George Bulwer-Lytton. He is the author forever linked to that dank opening line, "It was a dark and stormy night . . . "

The contest has been running since 1982. Please visit its website to enjoy other submissions, and submit your worst best offerings! The world awaits your wonders.

Whoa, are we at the end of the book already? I guess this ride is over. Sorry, but there's no use quarreling over it.

**MAN 1: Free-for-all. Mêlée. Donnybrook.**
**MAN 2 (slowly putting up fists): Those are fighting words!**

I have to admit I'm relieved, since I wrote this book longhand, and now I'm suffering from author-itis. And maybe this is the place to allow a slightly inappropriate Dad joke.

**Two soles wanted to go sightseeing. So they swam to the surface of the water and looked up, where they saw a pair of eagles flying overhead. The eagles (with their eagle-eyes) also saw the soles. "Ah, eagles!" said the soles, diving deep before the birds could catch them.**
**But the eagles were too polite to reply.**[2]

Thank you for joining me on this adventure. Again, I salute your courage and I appreciate the example you are setting for our youth. Admittedly, what we've talked about in this book is indefensible—but remember that playgrounds don't have plaques explaining why they exist.

That's because play—especially wordplay—never requires a defense.

---

2. If you are around adults and want the eagles to have a line, you can say, "Ah, soles!"

# ACKNOWLEDGMENTS

This book was made possible by Dad jokers in general and my father, Michael King, in particular. He provided me with years of excellent training in this field of study, and I'll never forgive him for it.

I'd also like to extend my sincere thanks to Bob Abbey, John Alkek, Kaden Anderson, Mark Atteberry, Dale Basye, Jordan Brown, Doug Downie, Emily Fuggetta, Bill Hamilton, Michael Hockinson, Quinn Horak, Alexis Howell-Kubler, Miranda Hubbard, Alaina King, Peter King, Donna G. Matias, Jaye Nasir, Jedd Parker, Scott Ryan, Chris Schmidgall, Suzanne Taylor, Lee Wassink, Jen Wicka, and the staff at the Multnomah County Library. I thank you all from the bottom of my pond.

A thousand thanks to my editor, Katie Killebrew. I was greatly impressed by her expertise, judgment, and forbearance with this project. And if you've read this far, I bet you are, too.

Finally, please don't ask my amazing wife, Lynn, what it's like living with someone who's writing a book like this. She's already suffered enough.

("Hey, Lynn, this is the last one, I promise. Tell me if this is funny . . .").

# SELECTED BIBLIOGRAPHY

My research was extensive and appalling. It led me into musty archives, dead-end alleys, and weird people's living rooms, and I regret nothing. The following sources were especially fascinating, and are recommended for anyone with a serious interest in this important topic.

Beck, Julie. "Why Do Puns Make People Groan?" *The Atlantic* (July 10, 2015).

Berkowitz, Joe. *Away with Words.* (New York: HarperCollins, 2017).

Farb, Peter. *Word Play: What Happens When People Talk.* (New York: Alfred A. Knopf, 1974).

Fetters, Ashley. "The Dad-Joke Doctrine." *The Atlantic* (Sept. 25, 2018).

Geary, James. *Wit's End* (New York: Norton & Co., 2019).

Jinsook, Choi. "A Linguistic Anthropological Study of the Typification of Middle-Aged Men in Korea: An Examination of Ajae Joke Data." *Korean Anthropology Review* (April 2018).

Johnson, Paul. *Humorists: From Hogarth to Coward* (New York: Harper Collins, 2010).

Mikkelson, David. "Death By Laughing" Snopes.com (Updated June 21, 2012).

Pollack, John. *The Pun Also Rises* (New York: Gotham Books, 2011).

———. "Bonfire of the Hannities." *Washington Monthly* (May 25, 2011).

———. "Here Comes the Pun: Why Wordplay Matters." *The Huffington Post* (April 9, 2012).

Redfern, Walter. *Puns* (London: Basil Blackwell Publisher, 1984).

Srinivasan, Narayanan, and Vani Pariyadath. "GraPHIA: a computational model for identifying phonological jokes" *Cognitive Processing* (February, 2009).

Tartakovsky, Joseph. "Pun for the Ages" *The New York Times* (March 28, 2009).

TV Tropes.com, online resource.

**BART KING** is one of America's top 100 Barts. As a child, he became fascinated with puns after learning that William Pitt the Younger (1759–1806) was so thin, he was nicknamed "The Bottomless Pitt." A longtime teacher, Bart has also written more than twenty-five books, and is a winner of the Bulwer Lytton Writing Contest's "Vile Pun" award. He intended to illustrate this book himself, but after drawing a blank, Bart was lucky to gain the assistance of Jack Ohman.

**JACK OHMAN** is the editorial cartoonist and associate editor at the *Sacramento Bee.* Ohman was a finalist for the Pulitzer Prize in 2012, and won the 2016 Pulitzer Prize for editorial cartooning. He has published ten books, many on the subject of fly fishing, inexplicably. Ohman has also won the Robert F. Kennedy Journalism Award, and virtually every other American journalism prize. It doesn't go to his head, much.